Decision-Driven Analytics

LEVERAGING
HUMAN INTELLIGENCE TO
UNLOCK THE POWER OF DATA

Decision-Driven Analytics

Bart De Langhe + Stefano Puntoni

WHARTON
SCHOOL
PRESS

Philadelphia

Published by Wharton School Press
An Imprint of University of Pennsylvania Press
Philadelphia, Pennsylvania 19104–4112
wsp.wharton.upenn.edu

Printed in the United States of America on acid-free paper

10 9 8 7 6 5 4 3 2 1

Ebook ISBN: 9781613631737
Paperback ISBN: 9781613631713
Institutional Hardcover ISBN: 9781613631720

Contents

Introduction
Divers and Runners

L et's start with a simple problem. There's no pressure here: It's just a way to set the scene.

Joey went to the store and bought a pack of chips. In this store, a bottle of water costs $3.00, a pack of chips costs $1.00, and a pack of gum costs $2.00. So, how much did Joey spend?

If you answered that Joey spent $1.00 because he only bought a pack of chips, you're correct. However, one in four individuals surprisingly answer this question with $6.00, incorrectly adding up all the prices listed. This error demonstrates a common problem: doing math just for the sake of it without considering the context.[1]

Now reimagine the same scenario with more intricate figures: *Joey went to the store and bought a pack of chips. A bottle of water costs $1.05, a pack of chips costs $0.75, and a pack of gum costs $1.70. How much did he spend in total?*

This reveals a curious insight. One-third of individuals now incorrectly sum the costs to $3.50, even though it is more difficult to calculate than $6.00. When the numbers involved are more precise, people are more likely to engage in unnecessary calculations.

Now, let's think about how this relates to the world of business and data analytics. Through our work teaching data analytics in business schools and companies around the world, we've noticed something. When faced with a business problem and a dataset, people usually fall into one of two groups: divers and runners.

Divers are those who love crunching numbers and can't wait to dive into the data. They see the dataset as a fun puzzle, and they're eager to solve it. But just like those who mistakenly added all the prices in the scenarios above, divers sometimes rush into statistical analysis without thinking about the business side of things.

Runners, on the other hand, feel the heartbeat of the business world. They feel the race against time, the constant push to make an impact, and the challenge of managing limited resources. They might not be best friends with math and data, but they have a knack for keeping businesses going. If you found yourself more interested in the outcome of Joey's shopping rather than the calculations, you might relate to the runners.

In business, data analysts are often like divers, while managers and decision-makers are often like runners. Sometimes, this can create an unintended divide, with each side failing to see the other's value. This lack of mutual understanding can make it harder for everyone to work together effectively. It can lead to misguided decisions.

When data is bigger, more precise, and complex, it has a different effect on runners than on divers. Runners might want to rush forward and focus on the immediate business goals, while divers may want to dig deeper into the data, unintentionally increasing the divide between the two groups. This is like what happened in our example, where some people were more likely to do unnecessary math when the numbers were harder, while others, the runners, became more likely to skip the math. The reactions vary, but the cause is the same. When data analytics becomes more intricate, divers plunge deeper and runners push harder.

For a business to do well, it's crucial to close this gap and encourage runners and divers to understand and value each other's skills and strengths. Effective decision-making in business requires a balance between decision-makers and analysts. To help with that challenge, we offer a new approach to using data for decision-making, which we call decision-driven analytics. In this approach, decision-makers play a more active role in data analytics, blending the best of both runners and divers to drive better business results.

Thinking Without Data

Picture yourself overseeing your company's car fleet. You've got two types of cars: SUVs that get 10 miles per gallon, and sedans that get 20. Each type of car makes up half of your fleet, and they all drive 10,000 miles a year. You've got enough money to replace one type of car with a more fuel-efficient model. So, should you replace the 10 MPG SUVs with 20 MPG ones, or the 20 MPG sedans with 50 MPG ones?

At first, it might seem like upgrading the sedans is a better deal. After all, 50 MPG is a lot more than 20, right? But actually, replacing the SUVs would save more fuel.[2]

Here's why: Right now, each SUV uses 1,000 gallons of fuel a year (10,000 miles divided by 10 MPG), and each sedan uses 500 gallons a year (10,000 miles divided by 20 MPG).

Let's look at what would happen if you replaced them: If you replace the SUVs, each new one would only use 500 gallons of fuel a year (10,000 miles divided by 20 MPG). That's 500 gallons less than before. If you replace the sedans, each new one would use 200 gallons a year (10,000 miles divided by 50 MPG). That's 300 gallons less than before. So, replacing the SUVs saves 500 gallons per vehicle each year, but replacing the sedans saves only 300 gallons per vehicle. Therefore, it makes more sense to replace the SUVs, even though the MPG number doesn't increase as much.

What this example seeks to highlight is the point that starting from the data you have isn't always the magic solution to making great business decisions.

Let's revisit the car fleet scenario again. You're in charge of a fleet of cars, and you're trying to save on fuel costs. You've got two types of cars, and one type could be upgraded. The difference is this: Nobody's telling you the miles per gallon for these cars. Instead, they're asking you what info you'd want in order to make your decision.

Now, your first thought might be, "Well, tell me how much fuel each car uses, or give me the miles per gallon." It seems obvious, right?

Sometimes the best answers come when we're not buried in a bunch of numbers. It might seem strange, but taking a step back from the data can actually help us see things clearer. That's the punchline of this whole thing: Thinking without data can, in a weird twist, improve how you use data to make decisions.

Why We Wrote This Book

Bart was trained as a psychologist and later moved toward statistics. Stefano was trained as a statistician and later moved toward psychology. Our paths crossed in the middle when we became business school professors.

Around fifteen years ago, the emergence of Big Data began to dramatically transform marketing. As a result, universities around the world launched new business analytics programs. Bart, then a budding assistant professor, was assigned to instruct customer analytics. He noticed that most existing courses focused solely on technical aspects, overlooking the vital role of behavioral science in decision-making. Determined to offer a more holistic approach, Bart integrated psychology into his curriculum, confident that this would better prepare his students to tackle business problems with statistical models.

Stefano later established a research center focused on AI and psychology to help disseminate the findings of his research among businesspeople. During his interactions with managers, he discovered a recurring theme: Analytics projects seemed to fail often, but hardly ever due to technical issues. The issues were always people-related.

In the past five years, we've taken our teachings globally through numerous executive programs. We aim to provide a fresh perspective on data analytics to business decision-makers. Most discussions on analytics tend to highlight data and tech prowess. This is understandable, given the rapid technological advancements, but the risk is forgetting about the business decisions that need to be made and the people making them.

Our approach to teaching analytics is counterintuitive because it pushes data to the background. It might seem odd to write a book on analytics through the lens of psychology. But our experience shows that the real game changer in improving a company's data usage is not acquiring more data or devising complex models. It is better integrating data into the decision-making process.

With the exponential developments in artificial intelligence, we see an alarming gap growing between managers and decision-making on one side, and data scientists and data analytics on the other. It's high time to put decisions squarely at the center of data analytics. Our hope is that this book will inspire you to do exactly that.

A Runner's Guide

Today's business world looks nothing like it used to. There's so much data, complex tools to handle it, and a growing gap between those who dig into the data and those who make the calls. This is why we need decision-driven analytics more than ever. We need to regain our focus on decision-making and the role of decision-makers, all while still making the most of modern data analytics. This is what decision-driven data analytics is all about.

We expect the need for decision-driven analytics to keep growing in the future. So, by reading this book, you're getting a head start. We're pretty sure that the businesses set to do great in the coming years are those that put decision-makers back in the driver's seat of the data analytics process. It's a must if you want to stay competitive. This book will give you the know-how and the tools you need, and it'll boost your confidence to kick-start this journey.

This book is a call to action, urging companies to refocus on the human decision-maker, the executive, the manager, the runner. While this book is about data analytics, it's not just for those crunching the numbers. Decision-driven analytics is built on foundational principles from psychology and decision sciences. Much of what we'll discuss in this book comes from that knowledge. What's new is how we apply these ideas to the modern world, full of data and evolving technology.

The book begins with a discussion of how decisions in organizations are often driven by the data available. Such an approach can result in analytics that don't align with business objectives.

From chapter 1 through chapter 6, we examine the essential components of decision-driven analytics. Central to this is the process of choosing the most suitable action from multiple options. There's a notable tendency for decision-makers to selectively use data that aligns with their preferred choice, an issue we confront in chapter 1. A more systematic approach involves first identifying possible actions, as detailed in chapter 2. These actions set the foundation for the ensuing analytics process. It's imperative to formulate clear and relevant questions to assess these actions, a topic covered in chapter 3. With a well-defined set of options and questions in place, chapter 4 dives into the actual data analysis. We address critical issues concerning data volume and the significance of understanding how the data was produced. Chapter 5 evaluates the answers that come from this analysis. It's essential to remember that no analysis can guarantee absolute certainty. Hence, answers must factor in inherent uncertainties.

In summary, decision-driven analytics focuses on "decisions," "questions," "data," and "answers," as illustrated in figure 0.1. Chapters 2–5 elaborate on these essential building blocks. Last, it's

Figure 0.1. Decision-Driven Analytics

worth noting that decision-driven data analytics has associated costs. Chapter 6 offers a framework to balance the costs and benefits of this approach.

This book will explain why decision-driven analytics is vital in today's world, where data is abundant. Our aim is also to guide you around common mistakes that have held back many organizations from using data to make more effective decisions. Throughout this book, we'll address key questions, such as:

- What are the shortcomings of the traditional data-driven approach to decision-making?
- How can adopting a decision-driven approach to data analytics enhance the impact of data analytics on business outcomes?
- Why is it crucial for decision-makers to play an active role in data analytics initiatives?
- Why is thinking without data the key to making better decisions?
- When should companies (not) invest in decision-driven analytics?

To answer these questions, we'll draw on our experience as teachers, consultants, and scientists. We'll be covering a wide range of topics: customer relationship management, digital advertising, personnel selection, political campaigning, financial valuation of brands, vaccine development, market segmentation, and much more. We'll be discussing cases across a range of industries, including financial services, technology, pharma, consumer goods, e-commerce, and automotive. And in the process, we'll be talking about gas stations, the London Whale Trade (spoiler: no whales involved), planets, and, of course, Elon Musk.

It's time for business to focus on the decision-maker and the core principles of decision-making. It's time to embrace decision-driven data analytics, a framework for combining the best of human intelligence and judgment with the power of modern data analytics and technology.

Chapter 1

Driven by Data, Decisions, or Preferences?

What has caused the gap between decision-makers and data analysts that we discussed in the opening of the book? We think it's tied to two major trends that have developed over the past twenty years.

Rewind to 2002. It was a significant year for behavioral science due to Daniel Kahneman, a psychologist, winning the Nobel Prize in Economics. He showed how our brains will often mess things up when we're making decisions about money. If you want to understand why we buy and sell things or how markets work, you must consider our brain's weaknesses. We aren't infallible decision-makers, and that affects everything in business and economics. Inspired by Kahneman's Nobel, more people got interested in studying behavioral science. It began to gain recognition and grew in popularity. More accolades followed, including a Nobel Prize for economist Richard Thaler. The big contribution of behavioral science is to focus the world's attention on the limitations of human information processing and the consequences of those limits.

The second trend is in computer science. Large tech corporations like Google and Microsoft continue to stun us with the capabilities of their algorithms, outperforming humans in more and more tasks. Consider the fast-paced development of artificial intelligence, with OpenAI's ChatGPT astonishingly reaching 100 million users within a few weeks. Add the emergence of groundbreaking technologies such as quantum computing, and it feels like today's news is ripped from the pages of a sci-fi novel. The devices we employ operate like data detectives, collecting vast quantities of information about us and our environment. What's truly impressive is their capacity to store and analyze this data at lightning-fast speeds, revealing patterns and associations.

Dismayed by the numerous examples in behavioral science of people's decision-making flaws and inspired by the many demonstrations in computer science of how computers achieve superhuman performance, many companies have started to prioritize "data-driven decision-making." They hope that data and machines can be an antidote to the biases of human intelligence, that they will improve business outcomes. Ask any CEO about effective management practices today, and data-driven decision-making will inevitably come up.

In Search of Engine Optimization

As algorithms grow smarter and gain more functions, they're finding more uses in the business world. Large language models, like that powering OpenAI's ChatGPT, can produce sophisticated text, which is useful in a variety of tasks. Take content marketing, for instance, which is key to digital advertising. This involves creating media to draw in customers. It often depends on search engine optimization specialists to create content that ranks well in search results, a process that can be challenging and time-consuming.

The process begins with understanding what content search engines prioritize, so that firms can produce similar content. The hope is that this content will rank high in potential customers' search results. While analyzing the top-ranking content is about crunching data, creating fresh content based on these findings falls on humans. But what if we could automate this?

A recent study gives us a glimpse into the future.[3] Starting with a keyword (like "IT service management"), a bot scrapes content from top search results. This content fine-tunes a large language model, which then generates new content mimicking the top results' style. Thus, the algorithm can create content similar to successful ranking content, reflecting industry-specific language patterns. A year-long trial found this semi-automated approach outperformed human teams in creating high-ranking content. The machine-generated content needed only slight editing, reducing content production costs by over 90% and greatly improving efficiency.

We Have It Upside Down

New awe-inspiring cases about the power of data and analytics like this one appear daily. And yet, a similar abundance of instances exists where the results of data analytics haven't been as hoped. The practice of data-driven decision-making, although seemingly straightforward, is surprisingly difficult to execute effectively.

Various executive surveys from renowned firms like Accenture[4] and The Hackett Group[5] have revealed dissatisfaction with the returns on investments in analytics. Strikingly, a survey from NewVantage Partners indicated that only around a third of organizations deem the role of chief data officer to be successful and well established. This feedback is particularly significant considering the respondents were chief data officers themselves![6]

The current situation in analytics can be bewildering. Many organizations invest significant resources and effort into analytics, with the expectation of favorable results. However, achieving success is not as easy as it seems. In an attempt to understand why, McKinsey conducted a study on unsuccessful analytics programs. The research produced a list of "10 red flags" illuminating the common causes behind these failures.[7]

The list includes issues like "The executive team doesn't have a clear vision for its advanced-analytics programs" and "Analytics capabilities are isolated from the business." Several other red flags pertain to a lack of clear goals, a lack of strategy, or a lack of attention to the implications of analytics initiatives. What's the common thread here?

The main problem appears to be not the technology but the way it is deployed and used. None of the red flags relate to the technology's capacity to perform its intended function. Instead, they highlight concerns such as a lack of vision, a lack of purpose, and a disconnect between data and decisions.

Instead of ten red flags, in fact, one could even argue that there is really just one big flag: Analytics programs fail when they are disconnected from key decision-making processes. This observation is further backed by the earlier mentioned chief data officer survey, where a mere 20% of respondents viewed technological limitations as the chief hurdle in becoming more data driven.

Companies often start investing in data-driven decision-making when they realize they have accumulated a vast amount of data and want to exploit it for business benefits. The idea is rooted in the belief that within this mass of data, there must be valuable insights that, when implemented, will enhance business performance. It is also perceived as wasteful to let the data sit idle. Essentially, the companies may be seeking to justify the resources they have invested in collecting and storing the data.

However, the downside is that this approach may create a mismatch between data analytics and the actual business decisions. In trying to find a purpose for available data, companies may end up focusing on irrelevant aspects or drawing insights that aren't actually beneficial to their operations or goals.

A significant issue with data-driven decision-making is its excessive dependence on the data at hand. Statistical analyses are executed to offer insights, yet these analyses might not reflect a comprehensive understanding of the available decision alternatives. Often, the spotlight is on the data itself rather than the decision and the critical questions that need to be addressed to make an informed choice.

Compounding this issue is the tendency for business leaders to entrust the data analytics process to data scientists. Although experts in data interpretation, these professionals may not always grasp the business dilemmas at hand or decision alternatives. This might lead to misinterpretation or oversimplification of the business problem being tackled, and analytics may thus fail to align with the strategic objectives of the business.

To put it succinctly, we have it upside down. Decisions shouldn't be data driven. On the contrary, data analytics should be decision driven.

Not Just a Way to Get Your Way

When we explain our approach of decision-driven analytics, some executives are quick to identify a potential pitfall. They rightly highlight that decision-makers who use data to substantiate a pre-determined decision may be falling victim to confirmation bias. However, that's not decision-driven analytics. Instead, it's what we call "preference-driven analytics," an approach that might be the most flawed way to make decisions, yet remains prevalent.

Let's rewind to 2020, when a lethal coronavirus paralyzed the world. Vast funding was funneled into vaccine research and development with the hope that an effective vaccine could be developed quickly. As the year drew to a close, pharmaceutical firms started to unveil findings from their randomized controlled trials, shedding light on the effectiveness of myriad vaccine candidates.

Randomized controlled trials play a crucial role in substantiating cause-and-effect relationships between interventions and outcomes, ensuring that the vaccines we use are safe and effective. In the case of COVID-19 vaccines, participants would be randomly assigned to receive either the vaccine (the experimental group) or a placebo (the control group). Control groups allow researchers to compare the effects of the intervention being tested against a group that does not receive the intervention or receives a different treatment. This helps to ensure that any observed effects are likely due to the intervention and not to other factors.

Pfizer and BioNTech led the announcements with an interim analysis of an ongoing randomized controlled trial. Their vaccine reportedly demonstrated over 90% effectiveness in preventing COVID-19. This percentage refers to the reduction in COVID-19 cases in the vaccinated group compared to the control group. For instance, an efficacy of 90% does not mean that 10% of vaccinated people will get the disease. Instead, it indicates a 90% reduction in disease incidence in the vaccinated group compared to the unvaccinated group. If the incidence of COVID-19 in the unvaccinated group was, say, 10%, a 90% reduction would bring the incidence in the vaccinated group to 1%.

The Gamaleya National Research Center for Epidemiology and Microbiology in Moscow followed, announcing that its Sputnik V vaccine showed 92% efficacy. Shortly after, Moderna announced its vaccine's 94.5% efficacy.

Then came AstraZeneca. On November 23, 2020, they presented interim analyses demonstrating their vaccine exhibited an efficacy rate of 70%—lower than those announced earlier by the competition. Ideally, they would have achieved an efficacy rate surpassing 90%, positioning their vaccine at the same level or possibly even surpassing their competitors. Imagine the disappointment the company must have felt with these results.

So, what approach did they take? They began dissecting the data in numerous ways and conducted a series of unplanned statistical comparisons. Within these multiple statistical analyses, they stumbled upon a silver lining. One of the two dosing regimens in their study—the half-dose regimen, which was tested on a subset of 2,741 participants, demonstrated a 90% efficacy rate.

Upon seeing this in the press release, we immediately sensed it wouldn't withstand scrutiny.[8] Why? Because this is an example of preference-based analytics. Continuously dissecting data will lead to statistically significant differences, purely by chance. AstraZeneca reported a total of 131 COVID cases among study participants but initially refrained from providing a breakdown. They later revealed that the 90% efficacy rate for the half-dose regimen was based on thirty-three confirmed cases: three in the vaccinated group, and thirty in the placebo group. These numbers confirm that AstraZeneca's vaccine is effective, but to assert that the half-dose regimen is superior to the full-dose regimen would be premature due to the limited number of observations. Furthermore, the dosage regimen variation was a mistake by a contractor involved in the study. AstraZeneca also later conceded to combining results from two differently designed clinical trials, one in Britain and the other in Brazil.[9]

AstraZeneca's approach is common; both academic and business researchers often make comparable mistakes. To make sound decisions with data, it's crucial to distinguish between "decision-driven" and "preference-driven" analytics.

With decision-driven analytics, we start by outlining the various options (in this case, different vaccine options). Next, we ask questions that help rank these options from best to worst. For instance, a question could be, "How effective is the vaccine?" The vaccine's effectiveness might not be the only factor to consider. Other factors like side effects, distribution hurdles, and production costs may also be important. Once we've framed these questions, we gather and analyze the necessary data to find the answers.

On the other hand, preference-driven analytics starts with choosing a favorite option (like declaring AstraZeneca as the best choice), and then hunting for data that supports this choice. It's not a recommended approach to analytics.

We once sat in a room, as consultants on a project, where a big strategic decision was being pondered. There were two options. One was to retain the current divisional brand and have it "endorsed" by the parent brand (a bit as in "Courtyard, by Marriott"). The other option was to fold the divisional brand into the parent brand and simplify. The boss clearly favored the second option, despite the concerns of others in the organization about the loss of brand awareness, and potentially also divisional autonomy, that this would imply. The organization had little data to assess the two options' relative advantages, and during the discussion it became clear that data needed to be gathered to make a decision. At this point, the boss wrapped up the meeting saying "OK, now go get me the data that shows I'm right."

We suspect that most readers have sat in similar meetings. Data shouldn't be used just to get your way.

Analytics, Powered by You

While data can help, it is ultimately the choices we make that determine our outcomes and impact the world. Decision-driven analytics is a significant shift from the conventional data-driven approach or the unfortunately common preference-driven approach. Instead of being primarily guided by available data, it emphasizes the decisions that need to be made.

Decision-makers must be at the center of data analytics. Decision-driven analytics aligns the efforts of data scientists with the highest-value contributions possible, directing them toward answers that impact decision-making, rather than letting them get lost in irrelevant data detours. Decision-makers are not merely tasked with accepting or rejecting data provided by data scientists; they also have to critically contemplate alternative courses of action and determine the necessary data for making an informed decision.

Decision-driven analytics is not about simply sifting through existing data for insights. It's about searching for specific data that can answer the questions we have—questions that stem from what we do not yet know. This approach highlights the strategic importance of what we don't know. It underscores the importance of intellectual humility and of challenging our assumptions about how the world functions.

It is worth emphasizing that decision-driven analytics doesn't mean that data mining and exploratory data analysis have no role in business. Many have argued that a crucial benefit of data-driven decision-making is the serendipity that can occur when we freely explore data. In fact, we have published several academic articles over the years where the initial idea came from observing a surprising anomaly in a dataset. There is often tremendous value in free exploration and data mining. But we take a different perspective here, by focusing on how data can help us make decisions. According to the decision-driven analytics framework, the first responsibility of business executives is to have a razor-sharp focus on their job and deliver on their key responsibilities. To do that, it works better to start from the decision at hand and work backward toward the data that is needed. Data mining and exploratory data analysis are valuable, but they serve a different goal.

The next four chapters flesh out the decision-driven analytics process by analyzing in detail each element of the framework: "decisions," "questions," "data," and "answers."

The Thinking Trap

The Trap

Let your preferences drive analytics.

What It Looks Like . . .

Decision-makers say, "Let's find the data that shows I'm right."

The Antidote

Decision-driven analytics highlights multiple courses of action.

The Takeaways

- Modern businesses are gravitating toward "data-driven decision-making," hoping to leverage data and machine intelligence to counteract human limitations and intuitions.
- However, many leaders find the outcomes of data analytics falling short of expectations.
- Starting from data that is available can create a disconnect between analytical outcomes and actionable business decisions. Even worse, often people start from a favorite course of action and collect data simply to confirm this is the right decision: preference-driven analytics.
- Decision-driven analytics puts decision-makers at the heart of analytics. Start by identifying potential decision alternatives. Pose specific questions geared toward facilitating informed choices. Only then, collect and analyze to answer those questions.

Chapter 2

Decisions

The leadership team at a global bank, responsible for client solutions, found themselves in a tangle with data analytics and approached us for help. Our task was to pinpoint the hurdles and develop a strategic plan to augment their data analytics usage. We applied a two-step method that began with a preliminary screening through a survey, followed by individual interviews for a more in-depth comprehension of the identified challenges.

The surveyed and interviewed executives expressed concerns about the company's data analysts. Analysts are invited to present projects at meetings of the leadership team, but their descriptions are often so technical that leaders lose interest. They found that the data was frequently too intricate and detailed, making the communication not straightforward enough. Several leaders suggested that additional coaching was needed to ensure effective communication.

However, our research uncovered a more unexpected and significant finding. The main roadblock to data utilization was confusion about decisions. Most leaders concurred that the leadership team included the right people and had a vital role to play. Yet, they were unsure about the scope of the decisions the team was responsible for and how these decisions were made. A few executives felt that the team was hardly making any decisions. As one executive put it: "We do not make any decisions. Discussions are not the same as making decisions." Another shared: "In our last strategic meeting, I don't think we made any decisions. But I don't know for sure. We reached some conclusion, but it wasn't entirely clear." Some felt that decisions were indeed being made, but they were unsure of who was making them or how they were reached. One executive noted, "The variety and scope of decisions is so wide that we get lost. We get lost in what we are deciding and who is responsible."

Some leaders suggested that decisions were sometimes made during one-on-one meetings and then given the nod in team meetings. Yet, there was a general sense of doubt about the actual purpose of these team meetings. One executive explained, "It is difficult to know if the purpose of the meeting is to inform, to ask for input, or to make a decision." Another added, "In the breakfast meeting, [NAME] presented something, but it wasn't clear whether the goal was to inform, or to get approval to roll out, or something else." The blurred lines between different stages of decision-making often led to confusion over what decision was made, when it was made, who made it, and how it was linked to prior discussions. Several leaders confessed their uncertainty about both the purpose of these meetings and their outcomes.

This situation, while unfortunate, isn't unique. Successful data analytics implementation hinges on a clear decision-making process. Before anything else, it's key to establish a list of decision alternatives. This list should contain only options within your control. If control is beyond you, for example, at a higher level, then the item shouldn't be part of your options. People are making decisions at all levels in the organization, and the decision options they can consider are constrained by their position in the organization. Pricing managers tasked with increasing margins for a manufacturer's website may assess that, ultimately, the best way to increase margins in the long term is to increase the quality of the products sold. This, however, would require improving the quality of manufacturing operations, which is not something they are able to influence. They may raise the issue with their boss and suggest the company makes moves in that direction, but there may not be much more they can do.

Once you have a list of decision options that you can control, you can start to consider the questions, data, and answers needed to rank these options. But how should you make such a list of decision alternatives?

Thinking Outside the Pump

A few years ago, we were invited to pitch an executive training program for a leading European chain of gas stations. They were struggling to optimize their brand portfolio due to the growth from successive acquisitions. We proposed to discuss a case study about Unilever's ice-cream business. Like ice cream, the gas station company's reaction was cold. They said, "What does ice cream have to do with gas stations?"

They were missing the point. You see, Unilever has faced similar challenges. They, too, had grown by acquisition and over time their brand portfolio had gotten overly complex, inefficient, and hard to manage. Unilever took a brave step, simplifying operations and creating a beautiful pan-European visual identity (the so-called Heartbrand), all while preserving legacy brands and valuable brand awareness across the continent. The gas station company could have learned a lot from this experience, but they were unable to see beyond their immediate gas station operations.

"Bounded awareness" often restricts our ability to see beyond a narrow range of options. We're inclined to focus on the most familiar or readily accessible decision alternatives, influenced by past experiences or immediate availability. Consequently, we often consider only a restricted set of alternatives for any decision—just a handful or even just one.

Diversifying Decision Alternatives

Maintaining a narrow perspective can limit the impact of analytics. Therefore, before diving into data collection or analysis, it's critical that we broaden our awareness of decision alternatives. We're not trying to list all possible options, but rather to formulate a feasible, innovative, and diverse set for analysis.

To illustrate this, consider the case of a car manufacturer that was aiming to enhance customer satisfaction with the car's audio system. The team managing the audio system was leading the project. They tried to address customer desires like "music should have a full, rich sound" by looking at ways to boost the speakers' or amplifier's quality. But these adjustments were pricey and hard to put into action. None of the options seemed especially appealing.

What would you have done as the project manager? Can you think of ways to improve customer satisfaction with the audio system?

By talking with customers and colleagues from the engine department, the team realized they were seeing the problem too narrowly. Customers often mentioned sound quality in the context of engine noise. This led the team to consider better engine sound-proofing as a potential way to enhance the audio system experience. This broader view allowed managers to spot a promising alternative that could be compared with more traditional solutions, such as better speakers.

Then comes the turn of analytics. The question is how much the perceived audio system quality is influenced by the audio system itself versus ambient noise. Analysts could run a study to evaluate this, by altering the background noise and sound system quality in a test room and asking consumers to rate the experience. Alongside budget and cost data, the results could be used to identify the most effective way to boost customer satisfaction with the audio system.

Effective analytics is rooted in decision-makers' ability to find high-quality decision options. When outlining the decision to be made, managers should think broadly about the choices to be evaluated. It's about casting a wide net and seeing what you catch. Doing so often involves talking to diverse individuals with different roles, backgrounds, and expertise. Decision-makers should challenge their assumptions and engage with people who might offer a fresh perspective on the problem.

For instance, the manager in charge of the car's audio system benefited from conversations with colleagues in the engine department. This calls for both a personal mindset and organizational culture that encourages seeking diverse viewpoints and promotes cross-functional collaboration and knowledge sharing.

Data analytics is more of a supportive tool than a final goal. It's meant to provide insights that steer decision-making. However, if our consideration set of decision alternatives is too narrow, it curtails the usefulness of our analytics. Hence, it's crucial to brainstorm about all possible decision alternatives before even beginning to gather or analyze data. The goal isn't to list every conceivable option, but to identify a wide and diverse set of practical options for analysis.

Feasibility of Decision Alternatives

Once we have explored possible options over a wide space, it's time to trim these down to a manageable set. It's often hard enough to gather compelling empirical support for or against one or two well-understood decision options. Asking decision-makers to now start considering a whole host of other options will quickly become overwhelming and paralyzing. But how do you trim the decision tree?

The first consideration is feasibility. Let's go back to the case of the car manufacturer trying to improve customer satisfaction with the audio system. The team could have considered other options. For instance, the company could have focused on the consumer instead of the car. One option might be to invest heavily in advertising. Lots of academic research shows that expectations shape experience. If consumers are convinced by glitzy advertising that the audio system is high quality, when they sit in the car they will be more likely to perceive the same sound as higher quality. This option is relatively easy to implement but very expensive to deploy in a mass market. If it becomes clear that this option is financially unaffordable, it shouldn't be in the short list of candidate options.

Alternatively, what if the firm could get drivers and passengers to wear headphones in the car? This would greatly reduce the impact of ambient noise and allow improving the sound quality at a much lower expense. However, this option has obvious issues related to safety. Because this option would never be implemented, it doesn't make sense to invest scarce resources in extensively testing it.

Impact of Decision Alternatives

Feasibility is not everything. Companies need to prioritize impact. This means the distinct alternatives should result in significantly divergent outcomes. It should matter whether you choose one option over another. When assembling a set of decision alternatives, decision-makers should ask: Will the choice between alternatives influence business outcomes significantly?

We once advised a company providing services to pharmaceutical firms. The company was considering ways to update their website. A web design firm recommended they start by examining how different features of the website could affect the behavior of site visitors, leading to actions like downloading product information or subscribing to an email list. It's easy to imagine the website differing along various attributes like color, font type and size, position of buttons, the amount of detail provided, and so on. The number of potential alternatives can quickly seem infinite, and it's not feasible to test every single permutation of these variables, especially for a relatively small company with limited resources.

So how should the company approach testing these design alternatives? The web design firm advised running A/B tests to see how different features affect visitor behavior. The company could create two versions of their website, one with larger font size and another with smaller, and conduct a randomized experiment. They could follow this pattern for other attributes as well.

While this approach works well for large companies with a high volume of visitors, it isn't always feasible for smaller companies. For example, the traffic to the website wasn't large enough to support many high-powered experiments. Smaller companies must narrow down the alternatives. We suggested the company adopt a more targeted approach. This involves relying on existing knowledge, industry best practices, and intuition to design fewer but more meaningful alternatives.

Imagine a scenario where the company is testing two radically different website designs: one with a minimalist approach featuring large fonts, light backgrounds, fewer texts, and more images; and another with a more text-heavy design, featuring smaller fonts, dark backgrounds, and fewer images. This approach creates starkly different alternatives that encapsulate different philosophies or strategies, rather than minor variations on a single attribute.

While this strategy cannot offer insights into the impact of individual variables, it provides valuable knowledge on larger strategic approaches. It's about testing the efficacy of overall concepts rather than getting lost in the minutiae of individual elements. Essentially, this approach treats each alternative as a comprehensive strategy or "big hammer," each with the potential to significantly influence business outcomes.

The Thinking Trap

The Trap

Start from the data that is available.

What It Looks Like . . .

Decision-makers say, "Answers must be in the data we have."

The Antidote

Decision-driven analytics starts from the decisions to be made.

The Takeaways

- Effective use of data analytics in decision-making remains a challenge for many organizations. While some leaders find data analyses too intricate, they also believe analysts need to communicate more clearly.
- However, the root issue often lies with the decision-makers themselves. Clarity is needed regarding which decisions to make, the designated decision-makers, and the decision-making process.
- Decision-driven analytics starts with a comprehensive understanding of the decision options at hand. Commonly, decision-makers gravitate toward familiar options. Broadening horizons and engaging with diverse perspectives can uncover a broader set of options.
- Decision-makers should focus on options within their control and pertinent to their organizational position.
- The choice set should include options that are feasible and impactful. It should exclude options with prohibitive costs or risks. It should include options that can genuinely enhance desired business outcomes.

Chapter 3

Questions

Subscription-based business models, where companies offer a product or service for a recurring fee, are becoming increasingly popular. The key in subscription-based businesses is building long-term relationships with customers, and this, in turn, requires proactive churn management. Churn, or customer attrition, can undermine the benefits of a subscription-based model by reducing the steady stream of revenue these businesses depend on. Therefore, businesses must anticipate, manage, and reduce churn.

Let's explore the case of Hewlett-Packard (HP), a corporation with whom we've collaborated on several occasions on the topics of decision-making and analytics. Over time, HP has incorporated subscription-based models into their business strategies. One of their successful ventures is "Instant Ink," where customers pay a convenient monthly fee to receive printer ink delivered at home. The flexibility of this model allows customers to discontinue the monthly payments whenever they wish, effectively ending their subscription. Naturally, HP aims to minimize this customer attrition, or "churn." In today's data-driven landscape, companies are increasingly recognizing the value of utilizing data to proactively address churn and retain their valuable customers. Now the question arises: How might HP prevent customers from discontinuing their subscriptions?

Churning Numbers

One tactic to decrease customer turnover is to offer targeted incentives. These could be a discount on the next month's charges or perhaps an extra item in their next delivery to persuade them to continue their subscription. However, given limited resources, they can't do this for all customers. So, they need to focus their efforts.

Let's consider three customers: Xiao, Yann, and Zoe. Who should HP focus on for proactive churn prevention? They could dive into their records and check each customer's subscription length. They might also tally how many pages each customer has printed in the past, monitor whether they paid for additional services like printer maintenance or fast delivery, and determine many other customer traits and behaviors.

However, having this data isn't enough. HP needs to know how these variables relate to churn. Useful comparative data would come from other customers who have already decided to cancel their subscription. By analyzing this information, HP can build a prediction model that relates churn to subscription length, printed pages, and extra service purchases. They can then use this model to predict whether Xiao, Yann, or Zoe is likely to churn. This is predictive analytics in a nutshell.

Imagine the model predicts that Xiao has an 80% chance of churning, Yann has a 50% chance of churning, and Zoe has a 20% chance of churning. Who should they target with an incentive, Xiao, Yann, or Zoe?

According to Wikipedia, "More sophisticated predictive analytics software use churn prediction models that predict customer churn by assessing their propensity of risk to churn. Since these models generate a small prioritized list of potential defectors, they are effective at focusing customer retention marketing programs on the subset of the customer base who are most vulnerable to churn."[10]

In other words, according to Wikipedia, HP should target Xiao, the customer with the highest likelihood to churn. What Wikipedia recommends has long been recognized as best practice in the industry. You build a model to predict churn likelihoods and then target your interventions to those customers who are most likely to churn. Common sense, right? Companies hate to see customers go and many aim to develop a "zero defections culture," as advocated in a classic article on service quality.[11] Naturally, that draws attention to the customers who are most likely to churn.

Question the Question

The data analytics we considered so far might not be answering the most important question for HP. The thing is, there are two different questions here, and they are easily confused: How likely is this customer to churn? And, what is the effect of our intervention on this customer's likelihood to churn?

So far, we considered how HP might utilize past data to answer the first question. They reviewed their customer records and created a model to predict if Xiao, Yann, and Zoe might end their subscription. This info can be handy for numerous decisions, but it's not the question they should be focusing on here.

HP is trying to figure out which customers it should incentivize to stay, so they need an answer to the second question. Budget constraints mean that they cannot provide an incentive to all customers. So, it makes sense to offer it to those customers that will be most positively affected by the incentive, right? These may be the customers most likely to leave, or maybe not. We just aren't sure. To answer this second question, merely reviewing past data won't cut it. HP will need to collect and analyze different data.

Ideally, HP had access to two identical universes. One where customers are offered an incentive, and one where they aren't. Comparing these two universes would give us a clear picture of the influence of HP's incentives on a customer's decision to either renew or terminate their subscription. However, given our current understanding of physics, such multi-versal comparisons are impossible. We're limited to observing a single universe.

HP's next best approach is to carry out a randomized experiment, also known as an A/B test or a randomized controlled trial, depending on the field. This technique is referred to as an "experiment" by psychologists, an "A/B test" in business, and "randomized controlled trials" in medicine. Regardless of the term, the concept remains the same.

HP would divide a group of customers randomly into two groups, akin to flipping a coin. Group 1 is presented with an incentive, while group 2 isn't. After this, HP would monitor for significant variation in the attrition rates between the two groups. If there's a difference, HP could then conclude their incentive made a difference. The key element of such a data-analytic effort is the random assignment of customers.

Marketing professor Eva Ascarza offers an illustrative example of the insights this approach can yield. She questions the widely accepted "best practice" of focusing on customers at the highest risk of discontinuing their subscriptions.

Let's look at figure 3.1, describing the results from one of her studies.[12] Customers are divided into ten categories based on the

Figure 3.1. A Randomized Experiment of Proactive Churn Management

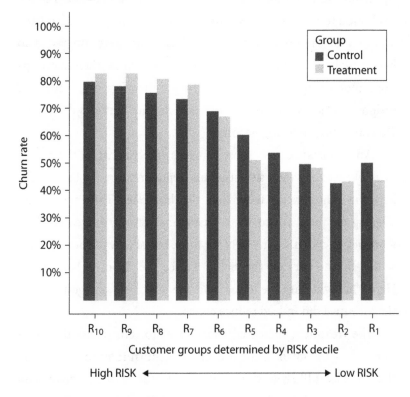

likelihood of canceling their subscriptions, as projected by a predictive model similar to what we previously discussed. Customers are ranked from the lowest 10% churn likelihood (the R1 group, on one side) to the highest 10% (the R10 group, on the other).

The two sets of bars, light and dark, indicate the experimental groups. The light bars indicate the customers who were "treated," who were given the incentive to stay. The dark bars instead indicate the control group, who received no incentive. The vertical axis, or y-axis, shows the actual observed churn rate for each customer group.

As expected, the bars generally slope downward from left to right, indicating a transition from groups with high predicted churn likelihood to those with lower likelihood. This simply confirms the accuracy of the predictive model—those who were forecasted to have a higher likelihood to churn do indeed cancel their subscriptions more frequently. However, the graph offers more nuanced insights. Let's take a moment to examine the light and dark bars. Do you notice anything peculiar?

An important observation from this graph is that for the groups most likely to end their subscriptions (represented by the bars on the left), the light bars are taller than the dark ones. This implies that offering an incentive to these customers actually increased their tendency to churn. Conversely, for those least likely to churn (represented by the bars on the right), we see the opposite happening. Here, the light bars are lower than the dark ones, suggesting that the incentive did indeed reduce churn.

The treatment increased churn rates for customers that were most likely to churn, while it decreased churn rates for customers that were least likely to churn. In other words, if this company had blindly followed the prevailing practice to target at-risk customers, it would have invested money to do the analytics, invested money on the incentives, and they would have lost more customers as a result! And without the data from this experiment, the company might have never learned how bad this approach really is.

Now, be careful. Your conclusion from this should not be to reverse the prevailing practice in the industry, and from now on target those customers that are least likely to churn. Professor Ascarza conducted a similar experiment at another company. You can see the results in figure 3.2.

Figure 3.2. Another Randomized Experiment of Proactive Churn Management

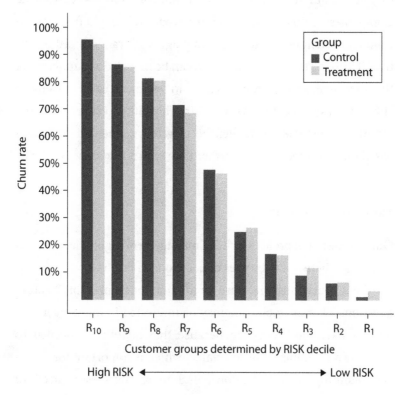

For this second company, the intervention successfully reduced churn for customers most likely to churn. If you glance at the left-side bars in the graph, you'll notice the lighter ones are lower than the darker ones. This indicates that offering rewards to customers who were at risk of leaving worked well! On the other hand, the same strategy led to an increase in churn among customers who weren't as likely to leave. If you look at the right-side bars in the graph, the lighter ones are higher than the darker ones.

The key takeaway is that it's crucial to conduct experiments to understand the impact of your interventions on customers. Companies aiming to manage churn proactively might first want to conduct a small pilot retention campaign with randomized incentives. Utilizing the pilot data, churn can be modeled as a function of the incentive and customer traits to estimate each customer's "lift"—the expected decrease in their probability to churn from the incentive. Customers can then be targeted in the full campaign based on their predicted lift, rather than churn risk alone.

Factual Questions

Our discussion of proactive churn management highlights a crucial distinction between two types of questions in business.

Some questions are pure prediction questions, or "factual questions." For example, one may be interested in knowing a customer's likelihood to churn because that quantity is needed to compute a customer's lifetime value, which is important for financial planning, firm valuations, and more. Businesses need to answer factual questions all the time. They provide crucial ingredients in all sorts of decisions. For example, smooth running of manufacturing operations rests on predictions about when a machine is likely to start failing such that a maintenance plan can be put in place.

Or think about the challenge of product returns, a significant hurdle for online retailers. These businesses leverage the online medium for its numerous benefits, including the potential for wider customer reach, reduced travel expenses for consumers, and cost savings associated with eliminating the need for physical retail spaces. However, these advantages are often offset by a prominent cost burden peculiar to online retailers, namely the cost of handling and processing product returns.

Pure predictive analytics presents a promising solution here. It would be incredibly valuable to identify which products have a higher propensity to be returned. With this knowledge, companies can strategize proactively, either by adjusting the product pricing, considering additional measures to reduce returns, or even deciding against offering such products entirely.

Recently, several fashion retailers have commenced an innovative approach to predict return rates by analyzing product images. They have begun to identify patterns, suggesting that certain colors, shapes, and other visual characteristics of products could potentially be linked to a higher likelihood of returns. This presents an exciting avenue for applying predictive analytics, further emphasizing its value and far-reaching potential in the e-commerce sector.[13]

Counterfactual Questions

Other questions require more than pure predictive analytics. They are about understanding the impact of interventions. For example, a company may be interested in knowing how an incentive will impact a customer (e.g., their likelihood to churn). We call these types of questions "counterfactual questions," because they involve a comparison between what would happen with versus without an intervention.

If analytics starts from the data that is available instead of the decision to be made, it increases the chances of confusing factual and counterfactual questions. Just like in the churn management discussion, that can lead managers to answer the former when in fact they should be answering the latter.

Another illuminating case is the 2012 presidential campaign, where Barack Obama and Mitt Romney contended for the presidency. Obama's winning campaign gained a crucial edge by framing political campaigning as a counterfactual question.[14]

The campaign's data scientists constructed models that prioritized voters based on their estimated likelihood of being persuaded to vote for Obama. Targeting the most likely Obama voters would have squandered valuable resources. Targeting hard-core Romney supporters would have similarly been a waste of resources. The most effective tactic was to pinpoint those voters most susceptible to changing their voting behavior when visited by a campaign worker.

By reframing the issue as a counterfactual question, the campaign could optimize its efforts and concentrate on engaging with potential swing voters effectively. This approach revolutionized the way political campaigns were conducted, emphasizing precision and efficiency in mobilizing supporters and persuading undecided individuals.

The lesson is the power of discerning between factual and counterfactual questions in decision-making. By understanding this distinction, we can harness the potential of data to support more informed decisions, whether in politics or other domains.

Fuzzy Questions

Today, when technology and computers are providing solutions at a click, we must shift our focus from getting answers to asking the right questions. This is what decision-driven analytics emphasizes. It underscores the importance of crafting the correct question as the primary, critical step in data analysis.

In many instances, businesses have squandered precious time and resources seeking answers to questions that were not relevant to their situation. It's crucial for decision-makers to distinguish between factual and counterfactual questions. However, it goes beyond that. Often, leaders and managers present questions to data analysts that are fuzzy, leading to difficulties in understanding exactly what is being asked.

We once ran a workshop with a European company that manufactures goods for household and professional applications. The aim was to enhance their utilization of data analytics. The workshop attendees included decision-makers and analysts. The decision-makers were asked to jot down questions they wanted the analysts to investigate. Here are some of the questions they listed:

- "How can we increase our gross margins?"
- "How can we manage our investments more effectively?"
- "Is the public engaged with [BRAND]'s brand purpose?"
- "How engaged are [COMPANY]'s employees?"
- "What goals do our customers have?"
- "What strategies are our competitors using?"

Let's consider the first question: How can the company boost its gross margins? This question is in fact not one to ask data analysts, but decision-makers. There could be numerous strategies to increase gross margins. As we emphasized in the previous chapters, decision-makers need to scrutinize these options and narrow down to the most promising ones. Only then should decision-driven analyses commence.

Some other questions are so broad that it's unclear where or how data analysis would begin to address them. Moreover, you might notice that several of these questions don't seem to be directly related to any specific decision. For instance, it's unclear what actions a manager would take after learning about the public's level of engagement with the brand's mission.

Fuzzy questions cause misunderstandings and delays for data analysts and can lead to frustration on both sides. Analysts can feel their work isn't having the desired impact, while decision-makers might feel they're not receiving the pragmatic support they require from data analytics, despite having skilled analysts and considerable investments in the field.

For data to serve its purpose, decision-makers need to thoroughly consider the questions they want to ask, honing them until they're precise. Conversations with analysts should involve clear, well-defined questions that lend themselves well to data analysis. Only after decision-makers have conducted their initial thinking without data should data analysts begin their work using data.

The Thinking Trap

The Trap

Fail to ask precise questions.

What It Looks Like . . .

Decision-makers say, "My questions are great."

The Antidote

Decision-driven analytics requires decision-makers turn their fuzzy questions into precise questions that can be answered with data.

The Takeaways

- A primary reason for dissatisfaction with analytics and miscommunication between managers and analysts lies in ambiguous, imprecisely formulated, "fuzzy" questions.
- Decision-driven analytics highlights the importance of crafting the correct questions that facilitate ranking decision options from more to less desirable.
- Decision-makers should first clarify their questions without data; only then should data analysts use data to find answers.
- Starting from the data that is available, rather than from the decision to be made, can result in "fuzzy" questions. This might lead to misconceptions, like addressing a counterfactual question as if it were a factual one.
- Understanding the difference between factual questions and counterfactual questions is vital. Factual questions seek direct information and rely on correlation-based insights. Counterfactual questions get into hypothetical scenarios, comparing outcomes with and without a particular intervention. They demand causal inference, making them inherently more intricate than factual questions.

Chapter 4

Data

In 2012, the world of finance was rocked by a scandal that became known as the "London Whale Trade," from the nickname of the trader at J.P. Morgan who caused it. The bank lost around $6 billion from a series of injudicious trades in credit default swaps.

A later investigation revealed that an important reason for the loss had been a typo in a formula inside an Excel file. Two interest rates in the spreadsheet had been inadvertently divided by their sum instead of their average, and this contributed to making volatility in the market appear lower than it was. The scandal led to the resignation of the chief investment officer and widespread criticism of the bank.

Many stories like this exist, where something as small as a simple typo in a spreadsheet caused disaster. When we rely on data to make decisions, it can make us vulnerable to mistakes when the data is flawed. That's why so much attention in data analytics is put into issues of data management and data quality.

However, oftentimes the problem is not data quality but the conclusions that are drawn from the data.

Meta Speaking Up for Small Businesses

On January 28, 2021, Apple's CEO, Tim Cook, took to the stage at the Computers, Privacy, and Data Protection conference. He delivered a significant speech focusing on the crucial need for user control over personal data usage in online advertising. Consequently, Apple updated its operating system to ask users for permission before businesses can track their data for targeted ads.

This decision stirred up Meta, then still known as Facebook, a company heavily dependent on personalized ads. They retorted with full-page advertisements in leading newspapers like the *New York Times*, the *Wall Street Journal*, and the *Washington Post*. The ads argued that Apple's move would harm small businesses. To facilitate discussions on the issue, Meta also established a dedicated website where small businesses could express their worries.

Meta claimed that the inability to use targeted ads would cause significant revenue losses for small businesses. "Without personalized ads," Meta stated, "Facebook data indicates that the average small business advertiser could lose more than 60% of their sales per dollar spent."

While it's a startling figure, you should not take this claim at face value. Understanding it necessitates a grasp of the metric used by Facebook for measuring advertising success. Return on ad spend, or ROAS, is a metric used in digital marketing to measure the revenue generated per dollar spent on advertising; it is calculated by dividing the revenue derived from the ad by the cost of that ad.

Meta, in its stand against Apple's policy, stated that small businesses could face a 60% revenue drop without personalized ads, based on ROAS comparisons. However, this doesn't tell us much about Meta's data-collection and analysis methods leading to this figure.

So, we penned an article in the *Harvard Business Review*.[15] In it, we argued that companies such as Meta should be cautious about making sweeping statements on the substantial impact of personalized ads, in the absence of evidence from randomized controlled trials.

By saying this, we're not trying to ignore the worries that many small businesses have about Apple's updates to its privacy policy. These concerns are very real. With Apple's new approach, companies need to explain how they collect data when they submit new apps or update existing ones. A lot of users probably won't agree to have their online behavior tracked, and this could affect how well advertising works.

Facebook claims it wants to support small businesses facing these changes, which is absolutely their right. But making big claims about how effective advertising is, without explaining how they got the data, isn't the right way to do it. Now, if the figure of 60% arises from randomized controlled trials, it definitely piques our interest. It's crucial to delve into the specifics and comprehend how this result was derived.

After the article's publication, Meta provided additional insights into their methodology. According to their statement, they conducted a comprehensive study involving over 25,000 campaigns across various industries and regions. These campaigns were categorized into two groups. The first group focused on link clicks and did not require any data sharing. The second group, labeled as personalized campaigns, was optimized for purchases and required data sharing. For these campaigns, Meta's algorithms identified likely buyers, leading to higher revenues per ad spend. However, it's essential to note that the higher revenues for these personalized campaigns do not necessarily imply that ads had a direct impact on people's propensity to buy.

Let's consider a hypothetical company with an in-depth understanding of its customers, enabling accurate predictions of their spending for the upcoming month. If this company targets its ads exclusively to high-spend customers, each advertising dollar invested is likely to result in substantial revenues, resulting in a high return on advertising spend. However, there's a crucial aspect to consider: These high-spend customers would probably generate significant revenues regardless of its ads. Their spending is driven by their inherent characteristics, not solely by the impact of personalized advertisements. Therefore, attributing all the revenue to the personalized ads would be a misinterpretation.

Small Businesses Speaking Up for Meta

After our article was published and our personal communications with Meta's public relations team, we noticed a change in their advertising approach. They began showcasing inspiring stories of small businesses that have benefited from their new services through ads seen at airports, magazines, and websites. You might have come across some of these ads, featuring businesses like My Jolie Candle, a French candlemaker that "find[s] up to 80% of their European customers through Facebook platforms," or Chicatella, a Slovenian cosmetics company that "attributes up to 80% of their sales to Facebook's apps and services," and Mami Poppins, a German baby-gear supplier that "uses Facebook ads to drive up to half of their revenue."

While these success stories seem impressive, it's essential for businesses to approach advertising with realistic expectations. The beliefs surrounding the effectiveness of advertising often stem from what tech giants like Meta or Google share in their "educational" materials for businesses. However, it's important to be cautious about drawing incorrect conclusions about the causal effects of advertising based on such information.

Let us illustrate this point with a case from one of our consulting clients, a European consumer goods company with a strong sustainability-focused brand. The company wanted to find out if an online ad emphasizing convenience would be more effective than one focused on sustainability. They used Facebook for Business to run an A/B test for both ads and compared their return on advertising spend. The sustainability ad performed much better—which means that's what the company should invest in, right?

Actually, we don't know. Meta's approach to testing, labeled as "A/B tests," has a fundamental defect that is not well understood, even among experienced digital marketers. Let's see what's really happening within these tests:

1. Meta divides users into two groups.
2. Within each group, Meta selects individuals and provides distinct treatments based on their group assignment. For instance, group 1 might receive a blue ad, while group 2 could be shown a red ad. However, not everyone in these groups will be exposed to an ad; hence, many won't see any advertisement at all.
3. Subsequently, Meta employs machine-learning algorithms to optimize its selection strategy. These algorithms may learn

that, for instance, younger users tend to engage more with red ads, leading to increased delivery of red ads to young people.

The implications of this approach become apparent upon closer inspection. The foundation of A/B tests is random assignment. However, can we consider the ad assignments to be truly random? No. And this aspect holds significant consequences. If we were to compare the treated individuals from group 1 to those from group 2, drawing causal conclusions about the treatment effect would become challenging. This is because the treated individuals from group 1 now differ from the treated individuals in group 2 on multiple dimensions, not just the treatment itself. For instance, the treated individuals in group 2 who received the red ad might happen to be younger compared to those in group 1 who received the blue ad. As a result, whatever this test may be, it cannot be considered a randomized experiment.

This problem is not limited to Meta; other platforms like Google also present misleading metrics. For instance, Think with Google suggests that ROI-like metrics indicate causation, but they are merely associative.[16] Computing total revenues from customers who clicked on an ad and dividing it by advertising expenditures gives a return on investment, but this lacks a point of comparison to determine the true impact of advertising on profits.

Scientists Too

Interestingly, it wasn't until after we wrote about the confusion over digital advertising analytics in marketing practice that we noticed the same kind of confusion had begun to creep into our own community of behavioral scientists. Over the past ten years, digital advertising platforms have evolved into significant data-collection tools for academic research. Numerous studies conducted on these platforms have been featured in top-tier academic journals.[17]

Several reasons make these platforms attractive to academic researchers. One is the vital role of randomized controlled trials in behavioral science. The objective of these trials is often to isolate the causal effects of a single variable from the plethora of other variables that may influence behavior. To reliably detect these effects amid all the noise, studies need to have substantial power. This involves gathering data from a large number of participants, a process that digital advertising platforms make easier.

Another reason relates to the practical relevance of our studies. There's an ongoing concern in behavioral science that our research may not fully translate to real-world scenarios. We often base our experiments on student samples from university labs or collect data from a more diverse population via online platforms like Amazon Mechanical Turk. However, these studies, typically based on hypothetical or oversimplified situations, aren't always reflective of reality. They ask participants to project how they would react to imagined or highly stylized circumstances, a task easier said than done. It's uncertain whether people can accurately do that. Digital advertising platforms provide an opportunity to study actual consumer behavior, often without participants knowing that they're part of an experiment.

In a well-known early study, researchers investigated whether marketing communications tailored to individuals' psychological profiles were more successful in swaying behavior.[18] The scientists conducted tests on Facebook using various combinations of target audience profiles and the personality of the advertisements themselves, aiming to understand if aligning these two factors could yield more clicks and purchases.

This is a big deal. The strategy, often referred to as "psychological targeting," has garnered significant attention over the past few years, particularly within the realm of political advertising. The 2016 Brexit vote in the UK and the US presidential election really pushed this issue into the public eye. The main debate was about foreign meddling in elections and how social media platforms might be helping bad actors try to change election results by influencing voters with specially targeted messages.

The study investigated how effective ads were when they were customized for Facebook users, using inferred personality traits from their "like" patterns. The researchers particularly focused on traits of introversion and extroversion. They categorized the audience's personality by targeting users who had previously liked topics associated with introversion or extroversion. For instance, a user who liked the reggae band Rebelution might be categorized as an extrovert, while one who liked computers might be considered an introvert. The personality of the ads was tweaked using introverted or extroverted design elements.

Remember when we talked about the "A/B tests" on Facebook? We mentioned a problem that could pop up: Could the targeting algorithm mess with the randomization of participants in this study? Essentially, we have to question whether users are truly randomly assigned to view ads that are either congruent or incongruent with their personality traits.

When everything is randomized properly, there shouldn't be noticeable differences between users who see congruent and incongruent ads on things like age and gender. But a detailed examination of the data reveals an unexpected age difference between these two groups, which is concerning.[19] This apparent lack of proper age randomization strongly hints that other unobserved user characteristics might not be randomized either, leading to uncertainty about what we can actually learn from this. We can't be sure if users who saw congruent versus incongruent ads behaved differently as a result of the psychological targeting strategy itself, or if it was because the people who saw matching ads are naturally different from those who saw mismatching ads.

What's Missing?

The randomized controlled trials undertaken by pharmaceutical companies in 2020 provided compelling evidence to suggest that the COVID-19 vaccines were highly effective. Israel was among the pioneers in implementing the vaccinations. However, many vaccinated individuals ended up in the hospital, which sparked worries about the vaccines potentially losing their effectiveness rapidly. Jeffrey Morris, a colleague from the Biostatistics Division at the University of Pennsylvania, decided to investigate hospitalizations in Israel.[20]

On August 15, 2021, Israeli hospitals were caring for 515 patients with severe COVID, 58% of whom were fully vaccinated. It may seem like a large percentage, leading some to question the effectiveness of the vaccines. However, there's a critical piece of information not included here, and that is the comparison of vaccinated to unvaccinated individuals in the general population. For instance, if everyone were fully vaccinated, then by default, all severe COVID patients would be vaccinated.

So, what's the ratio of fully vaccinated to unvaccinated people? Let's look at the number in table 4.1. There were about 1.3 million

Table 4.1. Professor Morris's Analysis of Israeli Hospitalization Data

Age	Population		Severe Cases		Vaccine Efficacy
	Not Vaccinated	Fully Vaccinated	Not Vaccinated	Fully Vaccinated	
All ages	1,302,912	5,634,634	214	301	
			0.0164%	0.0053%	67.5%
< 50	1,116,834	3,501,118	43	11	
			0.0039%	0.0003%	91.8%
> 50	186,078	2,133,516	171	290	
			0.0919%	0.0136%	85.2%

unvaccinated and 5.6 million vaccinated people. In the Israeli hospital case, 214 unvaccinated and 301 vaccinated people were in the hospital with severe COVID. That's 0.0164% and 0.0053%, respectively. Hence, the vaccine's effectiveness in preventing severe COVID-19 that is implied by these numbers is 67.5%. This percentage is significantly lower than the percentages reported by pharmaceutical companies earlier.

Does this mean the vaccine was becoming less effective? Not necessarily. These numbers don't consider age, a crucial factor in understanding severe COVID-19 cases. Older people are more susceptible and also more likely to be vaccinated. Ignoring age can skew our understanding of the vaccine's impact.

Let's look at the numbers again, but this time we'll take age into account. For people under fifty, there were roughly 1.1 million unvaccinated and 3.5 million vaccinated. Of these, forty-three unvaccinated and eleven vaccinated were hospitalized with severe COVID, which is 0.0039% and 0.0003%, respectively. So, vaccinated people under fifty were about 92% less likely to get severe COVID.

For those over fifty, there were around 186,000 unvaccinated and 2.1 million vaccinated. In the Israeli hospital case, 171 unvaccinated and 290 vaccinated people were in the hospital with severe COVID. That's 0.09% and 0.01%, respectively. Vaccinated people over fifty were about 85% less likely to contract severe COVID.

Oddly, overall data shows a vaccine efficacy of 67.5%. However, when we break it down by age, efficacy rises to 92% for people under fifty and 85% for those over fifty. This is an example of what statisticians call Simpson's paradox, where the relationship between two variables differs for the whole group versus within subsets of this group.

Here's the main point: We often use historical data to answer questions like "Is a vaccine effective?" or "Do personalized ads boost sales?" But it's important to think about what data might be missing. Adding that missing data could change what we think is true.

The Right Data

The solution to missing data seems straightforward: Stop it from being missing. Advancements in technology allow us to collect an ever-growing number of variables, which we can then include in increasingly complex statistical methods. The more variables we observe and include in our models, the closer we come to uncovering the truth. However, it's important to remember that what we're not observing often outweighs what we are.

Consider, for instance, studies conducted on online advertising platforms. Advertising researchers Brett Gordon, Robert Moakler, and Florian Zettelmeyer recently examined data from 663 large-scale advertising experiments on Facebook.[21] These experiments involved millions of consumers and resulted in a massive 38.4 billion ad impressions. Because these were true randomized experiments (not those of the flawed type we discussed earlier), the researchers knew the true causal effect of advertising for each campaign. The purpose of the study was to check if they would be able to recover these effects by using cutting-edge observational methods designed to extract causal effects from correlational data. The models relied on 5,000 user-level features. That's many more than advertisers or research agencies can get hold of. The team utilized a wide array of sophisticated techniques, like double machine learning and stratified propensity score matching. The researchers concluded that, even with all that, the observational methods were "unable to reliably estimate an ad campaign's causal effect."

Unfortunately, Big Data will often create a false sense of cause and effect. This was highlighted in an ingenious study conducted by behavioral scientists Joachim Vosgerau, Gaia Giambastiani, and Irene Scopelliti.[22] They asked senior executives to take part in a game in which they played the role of chief marketing officer of a restaurant chain. Their task? To choose whether to invest in Yelp ads or other marketing methods. To assist with their decision, they were provided with the results from two different studies about the effectiveness of Yelp ads.

In the first study, data about Yelp restaurants was gathered from the website and analyzed. The study included information about restaurants' reservations and advertising spending, and that allowed calculating the correlation between these variables. The second study was an experimental one, performed in partnership with Yelp, in which restaurants were randomly selected to display Yelp ads or not, and the number of reservations were subsequently recorded.

Surprisingly, the results of the two studies were inconsistent. According to the first study, restaurants that advertised on Yelp had 20% more reservations compared to those that didn't. However, the second study found no significant difference in reservations between the two sets of restaurants. It's important to keep in mind that the positive correlation between Yelp ads and reservations in the first study might not imply causation. For instance, successful restaurants might just have more money to spend on ads.

The intriguing part of the game was that the executives weren't aware they had been divided into two groups. Both groups were presented with the same two studies, but one group was led to believe the first study involved a massive sample of 12,000 restaurants, while the other group thought it was a mere 600.

When participants thought the initial study surveyed 600 restaurants, the majority trusted the results from the second study, with just a quarter choosing to invest in Yelp ads. These people recognized the value of a randomized experiment and doubted whether Yelp ads could truly boost reservations.

However, when the managers were under the impression that the first study covered 12,000 restaurants, two-thirds of the executives opted to invest in Yelp ads. This highlights a prevalent assumption that larger datasets are inherently more valuable. The researchers dubbed this phenomenon "the Big Data fallacy."

We are hardwired to explain what we see. Good explanations allow managers to prepare for the future and to take actions confidently, armed with the knowledge about the likely chain of events an action will trigger. This doesn't mean, however, that our explanations are always good, or that we cannot get better at explanation. Lightning is not caused by an angry god throwing a light dart from the clouds, like the ancient Greeks believed. The biggest cliché in data analytics is that "correlation is not causation." An association between two variables may indicate a causal relationship ("A causes B"), or it may not. Perhaps the association is causal, but the direction of causality flows the other way ("B causes A"). Or perhaps the correlation just reflects the association of the two variables with a third one ("B is correlated with C, which is correlated with A"), and there is nothing causal about it. Every executive knows this nowadays, but it is still easy to fall into the trap of thinking about correlations as causal.

Features of the data and the environment can exacerbate this tendency. We think this is an important element in how people think about the results of campaigns on advertising platforms. For instance, Facebook used data from over 25,000 campaigns to estimate the effect of personalization. It is easy to see how people will be impressed by this huge amount of data and take the causal claims at face value, even when they shouldn't.

Decision-driven analytics doesn't worship Big Data. Decision-driven analytics focuses on the right data to answer specific questions. Decision-driven analytics forces decision-makers to be clear about the nature of the data that is needed to answer a specific question. This leads them to reflect more on the data-generating process, which in turn helps them to make better decisions.

The Thinking Trap

The Trap

Take data at face value, especially Big Data.

What It Looks Like . . .

Decision-makers say, "Big Data is better."

The Antidote

Decision-driven analytics draws attention to the data-generating process.

The Takeaways

- Often, flawed decisions arise not from poor data management or data quality, but from our interpretation of the data.
- It's crucial to consider where our data comes from—the data-generating mechanism. Understanding this can shed light on missing data. Consideration of missing data can change conclusions.
- The solution to missing data seems straightforward: Just gather more data! This notion fuels the enthusiasm around Big Data.
- Cutting-edge technology enables vast data collection, which can be analyzed using sophisticated analytical tools. However, merely amassing data is counterproductive if it's not the specific data required or if it leads to incorrect conclusions.
- Decision-driven analytics prioritizes not just volume but the acquisition of pertinent data tailored to answer precise questions.

Chapter 5

Answers

O ne of the most surprising business news events of recent years was Elon Musk's announcement in June 2023 of the rebranding of Twitter, a company he acquired a year earlier for $44 billion, into X.

Twitter is one of those brands that are so well known that people turn the brand into a verb. Just like English people "hoover" the floor when they use a vacuum cleaner, people all over the world "tweet." Rebranding Twitter as X means giving up on Twitter's brand. And this brand is worth a lot of money. Elon Musk decided the rebranding was so important that it would be worth setting a huge pile of cash on fire.

But how big is the pile of cash exactly? To know that, one has to know the value of the Twitter brand. Many companies offer brand valuation services. They use a combination of historical data, customer surveys, and expert opinion to estimate the financial value of brands; that is, the net present value of future earnings attributable to the brand.

Bye, Blue Bird

Brands can be worth a lot of money because they often drive consumer decisions. For example, someone may buy a Volvo car at least partly because the brand makes them feel safe or because seeing the Volvo logo brings back fond memories. Perhaps they like another car model just as much, but because it's not a Volvo, they didn't buy it. The brand is many companies' most valuable asset.

The methodologies used by brand valuation companies are typically proprietary, so the details are not made public, and nobody knows how these valuations are made exactly, but the information available on their websites shows the methodologies to be highly technical, rigorous, and precise, estimating the value of brands worth billions down to the last million. For example, brand valuation firm Brand Finance estimates the Samsung brand to be worth $107 billion (ranking sixth in the world).[23]

In the case of Twitter, Brand Finance valued the brand at the more modest, albeit still significant, figure of $3.9 billion. That's a lot of money, but perhaps a loss that someone as fabulously wealthy as Elon Musk can suffer without big problems.

It is comforting to be able to provide a precise estimate of the financial implications of a particular business decision. But, in fact, nobody knows for sure how big Elon Musk's cash bonfire really is. Brand Finance's estimate is the lowest. Others estimate the value of Twitter's brand to be as high as $20 billion, or five times higher.[24] Perhaps even Elon Musk would be worried about the possibility of having burned an extra $16 billion?

Decision-driven analytics starts from the decision to be made, and that draws attention to unknowns, which is a major advantage. It makes it immediately obvious that there are limits to what can be known and that unknowns can be tackled in many different ways. For instance, if you tell people that Brand Finance has determined that the Samsung brand is worth $107 billion and ranks sixth in the world, most people will take this estimate at face value. Instead, if you ask people what they think the Samsung brand is worth, most will realize that brand value is a complex, multidimensional construct that can be quantified only imperfectly and in different ways.

They are correct. Kantar, another company making brand valuations, estimates the value of Samsung's brand at $32 billion.[25] That's less than a third of Brand Finance's estimate, a massive difference in both overall value and global rank (sixth vs. fifty-fourth). On top of that, while for Brand Finance the Samsung brand lost 7.1% last year, for Kantar the brand lost a whopping 40%.

Different companies are trying to estimate the same quantity but arrive at very different results. What are we supposed to make of this? The point is not that brand valuation is meaningless or impossible, but rather that brand valuation is a complex exercise that requires thinking in terms of statistical probabilities. Decision-makers can be drawn to precision, but this can breed a misleading sense of certainty. True business knowledge is not created by eliminating uncertainty but rather by embracing it.

Reflect on this: Are there instances where your organization has fallen into the trap of believing too strongly in precision? How does this affect decisions further down the line?

Missing the Target

The main goal of a business is to identify, satisfy, and retain customers. These customers are diverse, making business operations more complex. This diversity, however, gives companies a chance to stand out and meet specific customer needs. The marketing team helps businesses comprehend and cater to this varied customer base.

Market segmentation is the primary analytical tool companies use to navigate customer diversity. It's a process of splitting a wide market into smaller, more manageable groups. It's supposed to help businesses understand their customers, make informed decisions, and gain an edge over competitors.

Segmentation usually starts by choosing variables, such as demographics or behaviors. Data on these variables are collected through surveys, interviews, or data providers. After gathering the data, it's analyzed to classify customers into different segments. This can be a simple grouping based on responses to particular questions, or a more sophisticated multidimensional analysis using statistical methods like K-means clustering. Each segment is then profiled using characteristics like age, political views, or shopping habits, and the results are presented in user-friendly formats, such as tables or graphs.

To interpret these statistical profiles, marketers use techniques like segment labeling and persona writing. Segment labeling involves giving each group a descriptive name like "Urban Millennials" or "Minivan Moms." Persona writing creates imaginary characters that represent specific customer segments. These characters are based on the statistical profiles but aim to give a more in-depth look at each group. Elements like hobbies, family background, and career are included to make the personas more realistic.

These steps aim to offer a clearer picture of customers. However, it's worth questioning: Do these practices truly help businesses understand their customers better, or do they give a false sense of control? Consider the segments made by consulting firm McKinsey & Company presented in table 5.1.

Table 5.1. A Segmentation Analysis of Bank Customers

	Prosperous and Content	Deal Chasers	Financially Stressed	Recovering Credit Users	Self-Aware Avoiders
Percent of US credit card holders in segment	23	18	19	22	18
Median annual household income ($)	85K	65K	45K	45K	55K
Percent of segment with revolving credit card balance	29	81	93	64	64
Mean credit card revolving balance per household	890	3,802	7,453	1,726	1,969
Most-used instrument for POS payments	Credit	Debit	Debit	Debit	Cash
Share of credit card in POS spending	59	24	20	11	19
Most-used credit card does not earn rewards	8	37	52	45	43

Fiorio, L., R. Mau, J. Steitz, and T. Welander, "New Frontiers in Credit Card Segmentation: Tapping Unmet Consumer Needs," *McKinsey Report* (2014). Retrieved August 7, 2023, from https://www .mckinsey.com/~/media/mckinsey/dotcom/client_service/financial%20services/latest%20thinking /payments/mop19_new%20frontiers%20in%20credit%20card%20segmentation.ashx.

McKinsey consultants already gave the segments names like "Prosperous and Content" and "Deal Chasers." Now, let's craft personas for these segments. What might they look like? Are they married? Where do they live? What hobbies or sports do they engage in? What does an average day in their life entail?

For the first segment, we might envision someone like "Beaches," a happily married violinist who adores her work and her spouse, enjoying the quiet pleasures of late-night movies and relaxation.

he "Deal Chasers," we could picture "Jersey," a fresh
ing on parental support who enjoys maintaining his
 and hanging out with friends.

Will these personas improve understanding of customer needs? Will they help make more accurate predictions about customer behavior? How do they affect marketing decisions?

To answer these questions, we conducted studies with hundreds of participants, in collaboration with Quentin André and Philip Fernbach, marketing professors at the University of Colorado at Boulder. The personas "Beaches" and "Jersey" were devised by one of our participants.

Our findings were surprising. The creation of segment names and personas actually muddied the understanding of customer diversity.

One of the things we looked at was how managers perceived differences between average customers from different segments. Results showed that segment naming and persona writing exaggerate perceived differences between segments. This is what we call the amplification effect.

We also examined how managers perceived differences between customers from the same segment. Here, we found a compression effect. After participants named segments or wrote personas, perceived differences within segments were smaller. These amplification and compression effects reduced the accuracy of behavioral predictions and influenced marketing decisions like email campaign targets.

What we can conclude from our research is that the standard segmentation process may not necessarily deepen our understanding of customer diversity but, rather, could obfuscate its complexities. The risk is that the hunt for precision in segmentation analysis blinds us to the subtleties of consumer behavior.

The difficulties aren't just linked to the way we label segments or create personas. Consider, for example, when we profile segments a~

shown in table 5.1. We usually use averages, but this overlooks the spread or variation. This can oversimplify things, making the differences between groups seem larger and the differences within segments seem smaller than they really are. In fact, the same data could be grouped in countless ways. There's no absolute, single "correct" solution. And when you settle on particular clusters, the differences within these groups are frequently far more substantial than the differences between the clusters themselves.

Visual Illusions

Analysts will sometimes use visuals like graphs to help managers understand statistical groupings. But these visuals can make matters worse. The fact is, people are unique. This diversity can be represented in various ways, and the way it's portrayed can significantly influence the conclusions managers draw.[26]

Take figure 5.1 as an example. It shows the same dataset in two distinct ways. The dots indicate the average of two segments for a spending index in a product category. The dots remain constant

Figure 5.1. Two Different Visualizations of the Same Data

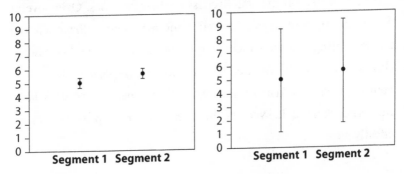

across both sections of the figure. The difference lies in the error bars around the dots.

On the left, variance is shown using a statistical index that underscores group differences (based on standard errors). Much like the case of segment naming, this amplifies the differences. On the right, variance is shown instead through a statistical index highlighting differences within groups (based on standard deviations).

Despite displaying identical data, the conclusions drawn from each figure can be strikingly different. From the left figure, one may think that the segmentation is useful and that the two segments spend significantly different amounts in the category. From the right figure, however, one might come to the opposite conclusion: The segmentation isn't very useful, because there is more diversity within each segment than between them.

Usually, when creating this sort of graph, the default is to use error bars like those on the left. This can make the differences between groups seem larger than they are, potentially leading managers to make decisions based on misguided assumptions.

Understanding Versus Convincing

We previously talked about pharmaceutical companies and how they've reported on the effectiveness of their vaccines. Over several weeks, multiple firms made their announcements. Pfizer led the charge, stating that their vaccine was "over 90% effective." Following closely, the Gamaleya Center in Moscow reported that their Sputnik V vaccine had shown "92% effectiveness." Five days later, Moderna claimed its vaccine had reached an impressive "94.5% effectiveness."

Did you pick up on anything interesting? These percentages are becoming more and more precise. The Gamaleya Center gave us "92%," not just "over 90%," while Moderna declared "94.5%" instead of rounding to "94%."

What's the reason for this precision? We can't say for sure, but it's possible these companies believed that exact numbers would bolster confidence and also highlight their edge over Pfizer. This maneuver paid off. For instance, the Belgian newspaper *De Standaard* wrote that "the candidate vaccine of the American biotech company Moderna works even better than that of Pfizer."

Precise figures have a compelling effect. Donald Trump tapped into this during his presidency, when he tweeted "We are not even into February and the cost of illegal immigration so far this year is $18,959,495,168. Cost Friday was $603,331,392. There are at least 25,772,342 illegal aliens, not the 11,000,000 that have been reported for years, in our Country. So ridiculous! DHS." By contrasting his precise figures about illegal immigration with the round numbers provided by the Department of Homeland Security (DHS), he may foster greater trust in his own statistics.

To make smart choices, it's crucial to distinguish between times when you're trying to understand how the world works and when you're working to convince others about your worldview. In the first case, when the goal is to understand, you should focus on getting a grip on the unknowns. In the second case, where you are trying to convince others, being precise can really help.

When you're trying to understand the world and you encounter specific figures, don't rush to think that more detail means better insights. Instead, ask for a range to better judge how reliable those numbers are. Knowing that a vaccine's effectiveness can vary from

70% to 95%, or a brand's value could be anywhere between \$30 and \$110 billion, gives you a more realistic understanding of what's going on.

In the same way, be mindful of the categories your mind imposes on the world. Categorical thinking often leads to misconceptions, as we discussed in the context of segmentation.[27] For a classification system to be valuable, it needs to satisfy two criteria: First, it needs to be valid. In other words, it can't arbitrarily split an otherwise homogeneous group. Valid classifications, as Plato suggested, "cut nature at its joints"—like distinguishing between snakes and sticks. Secondly, it must be useful, meaning the different categories should behave differently in ways that are significant to us. Identifying a snake from a stick could potentially save your life during a forest walk.

However, in business, we often rely on categories that may be invalid, unhelpful, or both. This can lead to substantial mistakes in decision-making. Take the Myers–Briggs Type Indicator, a widely used personality assessment tool that is reputedly used for HR decisions in over 80% of Fortune 500 companies. This tool classifies individuals into one of sixteen personality types based on their responses to ninety-three questions. The issue is these questions call for complex, ongoing evaluation. For example, a question like, "Do you rely more on facts or intuition?" would lead many of us to respond, "It depends." But the test doesn't provide that as an option. Consequently, people have to choose between one option or the other, leading to classifications that may not accurately represent them. Besides, these categories are not particularly valid or useful; for instance, personality type is often a poor predictor of important outcomes such as job satisfaction or success.[28]

Fussy Questions, Fuzzy Answers

Does the idea of being labeled "fussy" or "fuzzy" appeal to you? Probably not. Both terms generally carry negative connotations.

A "fussy" individual tends to obsess over minor details, making them difficult to satisfy. The spectrum of fussiness might range from a baby who cries at the smallest discomfort to a diner who sends back their meal because it's not to their liking. Being fussy implies a demanding nature, often causing annoyance or inconvenience to others.

On the flip side, a "fuzzy" person is often vague in their communication. Their responses lack specificity, leaving ample room for interpretation. For example, if you ask about their weekend plans, they might ambiguously reply, "Not sure, maybe just chilling." This, too, isn't particularly appealing.

While we typically avoid associating with either fussy or fuzzy personalities, the realm of decision-driven analytics interestingly welcomes these traits.

In this context, a "fussy" approach is crucial for decision-makers when they ask questions. It suggests a meticulous and precise mindset, which is beneficial when formulating questions. A good question is clear, focused, and well structured, and it often requires a careful consideration of what exactly you're trying to find out.

Conversely, data analysts should embrace a "fuzzy" approach when providing answers. In the realm of computer science, "fuzzy" implies a partial truth, a concept that accepts a certain level of uncertainty in the accuracy of any given answer. Often, people making decisions feel more confident when data analysts present answers that are superprecise. But this isn't always the right way to think about it. The world is a messy, unpredictable place. So, answers that reflect this messiness are actually more true to life.

Commonly, decision-makers ask fuzzy questions and expect fussy answers. However, a more effective approach would be the exact opposite: Ask fussy questions and anticipate fuzzy answers.

The path to understanding isn't a straight line but rather a dynamic process of constant questioning and answering. "Fuzzy" answers have another benefit: They lead to more precise questions. For instance, the discovery of quantum mechanics—providing a "fuzzy" answer to the behavior of particles at a very small scale— has led to precise questions about the nature of quantum entanglement, superposition, and other phenomena.

In college, while studying statistics, we often spent time fitting statistical models to data. We mostly worked on phenomena related to biology and the natural sciences. Predicting the growth of fruit flies in a jar with near-perfect accuracy was quite rewarding. But things took a different turn when we started gathering data about people's preferences for our final research project. The statistical models didn't perform so well; their predictive power was a mere shadow of what we had seen before. It turns out that people are a whole lot more complicated than fruit flies.

Predicting human behavior is tough. The human brain is a complex web of neurons, and adding social connections to the mix just complicates things further. Trying to anticipate what people will do can be baffling and even make you question the value of business studies and detailed plans.

But we need to embrace this complexity to make smart choices. Decision-driven analytics requires a dose of humility. It means realizing that our predictive abilities have limits. Decision-makers need to admit there's a lot they don't know and accept that not everything can be predicted. While this might be a tough realization, we need to accept the world as it is. This doesn't mean we should ditch data analytics. Decisions grounded in strong evidence usually turn out to be the better ones.

The Thinking Trap

The Trap
Seek out precise answers.

What It Looks Like . . .
Decision-makers say, "Data analysts should give precise answers."

The Antidote
Decision-driven analytics values fuzzy answers that acknowledge complexity.

The Takeaways

- We inherently gravitate toward clear, precise answers because they instill a sense of understanding and control over our environment. Yet, the complexity and unpredictability of the world mean we cannot eradicate all uncertainty.
- Precise answers can be useful when trying to convince others. But when the goal is to understand, it's essential that answers acknowledge and embrace uncertainty.

- Rigid, categorical thinking can misguide our answers. For a classification system to be valuable, it must be both valid, meaning it accurately distinguishes between distinct groups, and useful, ensuring these distinctions have meaningful implications.

Chapter 6

Data for a Purpose

We were once invited to a multinational company's main office to discuss their brand-tracking study. The brand team had been consistently conducting the same survey across their major markets, covering about a dozen countries. The survey tackled various topics, such as brand liking, emotional responses, brand personality, and core associations. This had been an ongoing collaboration with an agency for years, involving detailed surveys with a broad spectrum of global consumers every quarter. It wasn't cheap.

The challenge was that the results hardly showed any significant changes from one quarter to the next. Moreover, the slight changes that did appear seemed random and weren't part of a consistent trend. Despite any marketing efforts made by regional offices, the metrics weren't budging.

The brand was already well known in these markets. The metrics, largely based on long-term memory and perceptions, were generic. The consumers surveyed weren't necessarily those impacted by specific marketing campaigns, like a local sports event sponsorship. Given these circumstances, we observed that it would be tough to pinpoint shifts in perception. They had invested heavily in gathering this data but struggled to derive actionable insights from it. When asked about the reason for the continuous study, the answer was simply, "It's what we've always done."

While the team recognized the inefficiency of their approach, discontinuing the study wasn't straightforward. The data did provide some value for comparisons—either between countries or against competitors. However, they might not need to gather it as frequently in every country. It's possible that the funds could be more effectively used on targeted research, focusing on specific audiences or products.

This scenario underscores a prevalent issue: While managers often grapple with finding valuable insights from regular tracking studies, it's equally challenging for them to halt long-standing projects.

The Metric Bandwagon

Often, the data chosen for collection mirrors prevailing trends rather than thoughtful and strategic planning. For instance, many marketing managers jump on the bandwagon of the latest metric, medium, or technology simply because it's the "in thing."

Consider the current trend: Numerous businesses are utilizing the net promoter score (NPS), which gauges if customers would recommend their brand to others. Many companies adopt this metric without pausing to reflect on its relevance for their specific context.

Overreliance on popular metrics like NPS can give a skewed perspective on customer satisfaction and loyalty. When every company in an industry zeroes in on a single metric, they might overlook other crucial data points. Such a narrow focus can lead to missed opportunities, misallocated resources, and strategic errors.

Applying a generic approach to customer research can be detrimental. Each customer's experience, needs, and expectations vary, necessitating tailored questions. Additionally, the significance of certain questions can evolve, particularly in rapidly changing industries. Asking different questions at different points in time can yield invaluable insights that can shape the direction of a company's strategy and operations.

Moreover, repeatedly bombarding customers with identical questions can be off-putting. It can convey indifference, reflecting a superficial engagement with their experience. Instead of blindly adhering to industry norms, businesses should periodically reevaluate the questions they ask.

Decision-driven analytics isn't just about crunching numbers. It's about making sure that when we use data, it helps the company make better choices that fit its goals. Before diving into the data, we should check if the answers we get will really help the business. Finding answers takes time and money, and it doesn't make sense to find answers for everything. That's just overwhelming.

So, decision-makers need to think about when it's best to look for answers. To make sure they're using their resources wisely, companies should consider three questions before putting in time and money:

- How big of a deal is the decision?
- Is the question really relevant?
- How much will it cost to collect and analyze the data?

Let's examine each.

The Impact of the Decision

Imagine you're a manager in charge of office supplies for your department. The supplier offers sticky notes in two colors: pastel blue and pastel yellow. Both colors cost the same, are available in the same quantities, and have the same adhesive quality. While some employees might have a slight preference for one color over the other, the color of the sticky notes used internally won't affect their core functionality. Furthermore, the color won't influence any external business operations or customer perceptions. Given these factors, it wouldn't make sense to conduct a survey among employees or invest in analytics to determine which color to order. A simple executive decision based on whatever color the manager feels like ordering (or even random choice) would suffice.

Before investing in analytics, it is critical to understand the potential consequences of our choices—both positive and negative. Many decisions do not have enough impact to warrant detailed analysis.

Unfortunately, within organizations, individuals can become preoccupied with minor details, diverting time and resources from more pressing matters. For instance, we sometimes find ourselves spending way too much time on details like the selection of a Power-Point font or the inclusion of a specific picture. Similarly, pondering endlessly over the choice of an email header may consume more time than necessary.

Decision-driven data analytics requires prioritizing our efforts and avoiding getting mired in inconsequential analytics initiatives.

The Relevance of the Question

The impact of a decision isn't the only factor to consider. It's also essential to gauge whether the question you aim to answer with analytics helps make a well-informed ranking of decision alternatives.

Questions that come to mind easily are not always the ones that need an answer. Remember the HP proactive churn management case from chapter 3. There were two questions:

1. How likely is a customer to churn?
2. What impact does an intervention have on a customer's likelihood to churn?

Though these questions seem connected, only the second one was relevant in that context. The decision of whether to target a customer with an intervention is vital. But determining the mere likelihood of a customer's churn isn't pertinent to that choice.

Oftentimes, the questions we ask are inspired by the data we have, but they may not be the most relevant to the decision to be made. Imagine an HR manager wants to boost employee productivity and is debating offering employees the option to work from home either one day per week or two days per week. In this scenario, one might ask questions such as: How many hours are employees logged in? How many emails do employees send?

While there is a plethora of data that might be considered, not all of it is relevant when deciding on the number of work-from-home days to offer employees. Simply being logged in to work-related systems or platforms doesn't mean an employee is productive. It could just be that they left a system running or forgot to log out. On the surface, if employees are sending more emails, it might seem like they're more active or engaged. However, more emails could indicate inefficiencies, miscommunication, or even just spam.

Instead of concentrating on these readily available, but potentially misleading, metrics, the HR manager should strive to understand the true essence of productivity by asking questions such as: Are employees producing quality work? Are tasks and projects being completed efficiently and effectively? Are employees feeling more motivated and less stressed when working from home? Furthermore, it's also critical to consider the intangible benefits of allowing employees to work from home. Such benefits might include improved employee morale, reduced commuting stress, increased job satisfaction, and even potential cost savings for the company in terms of reduced office space and overhead.

Determining whether to seek an answer involves critically assessing the question's relevance. Distinguishing between relevant and irrelevant questions can be challenging.

This challenge is starkly evident in promotion decisions. Consider the Peter Principle, which posits that employees tend to get promoted until they reach a position where they're no longer effective.[29] The basis for promotions often revolves around an individual's performance in their existing role, rather than their aptitude for the next. Consequently, this could lead to positions being occupied by individuals not best suited for them. For instance, a study on US sales workers highlighted that companies often prioritize current job performance over future managerial potential during promotions. This results in top-performing salespeople being promoted over those who might possess superior managerial capabilities.[30]

A similar conundrum exists in academia. Professors are often awarded tenure based largely on their success in publishing in esteemed journals. However, senior academic roles demand skills like mentorship and leadership—skills that might not align with the specialized and technical prowess needed for top-tier journal publications.

So, when considering an employee for a potential promotion, the relevant question is not how well they perform in the current position. The relevant question is how well they're going to perform in the new position.

The Cost of the Data

Finally, even when the decision is important and the question is relevant, you might conclude that data analytics would be too expensive. The issue here is with the data.

It's possible that even for very important decisions, acquiring the relevant data might be too expensive or time-consuming. This could be due to the methods needed, the rarity of the data, or the resources required. The cost must be weighed against the potential benefits or consequences of the decision.

Surveys, often distributed in the form of questionnaires, are a popular method to gather data. They can be disseminated to a large audience at relatively low costs, especially if done online. However, the quality of the data might vary depending on how the survey is designed and administered.

Experiments provide a more controlled environment to gather data. They can yield deeper insights, especially on causal relationships. However, they are usually more costly than surveys. This is because they often require specialized equipment, locations, personnel, and more time to ensure that variables are controlled and results are accurate.

Online experiments, especially in the age of digital marketing and A/B testing, can be scaled easily. For example, a website might test two different homepage designs to see which leads to more user engagement. This can be done relatively inexpensively. In contrast, offline experiments, say in a physical store or a laboratory, may require more resources in terms of equipment, personnel, and logistics.

Also, what's considered expensive is context dependent. It can vary based on a company's financial health, size, and priorities. For instance, the cost and potential returns of any business decision, like A/B testing different button colors, are heavily influenced by scale. For a smaller company, the marginal return on such tests might be insignificant, especially when considering the time and resources needed to conduct the test properly and interpret the results. If they only get fifty website visitors a day, it might take a prohibitively long time to gather enough data to determine a statistically significant difference between the green and blue buttons.

On the other hand, a large e-commerce site with millions of visitors can gather significant data much faster. The same test that would take months for a small company could be accomplished in a day or two for a large company. Moreover, larger companies might have more specialized teams and a culture of continuous testing and optimization. For them, running such tests might be part and parcel of their regular operations. Smaller companies might not have the same expertise or might prioritize other activities that yield more immediate and tangible benefits.

Putting It Together

Decision-driven analytics is a strategic approach that emphasizes the alignment of analytical efforts with decision-making needs. As

Figure 6.1. Should We Do Data Analytics?

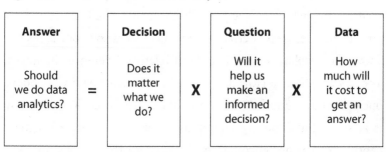

Answer		Decision		Question		Data
Should we do data analytics?	=	Does it matter what we do?	X	Will it help us make an informed decision?	X	How much will it cost to get an answer?

we've covered in previous chapters, decision-driven analytics hinges on four parts: the decision itself, the question we aim to answer, the data we use, and the answer we derive. While it's tempting to dive into data analysis, it's essential to first determine if the answer that comes out of the analysis will truly impact business objectives.

It's useful to consider these four components as variables that need estimation. You could envision these quantities interconnected in a way that they multiply to give:

$$(\text{Desire to Seek}) \text{ Answer} = \text{Decision} \times \text{Question} \times \text{Data}$$

In this equation, "Answer" reflects when analytics should be employed. It is a function of the other three variables. "Decision" represents the decision's significance for the business ("Does it matter what we do?"). "Question" signifies the usefulness of the question in making a choice ("Will it help us make an informed decision?"). "Data" indicates how hard it is to find an answer to the question using data ("How much will it cost to get an answer?"). See figure 6.1 for a representation of this equation.

Applying the Formula

Let's look at how we can score these elements: Decision, Question, and Data. We'll use a scale of 0, 1, or 2 for simplicity.

For Decision, a score of 0 implies low impact, 1 suggests a medium impact, and 2 suggests a high impact. The focus is on how your choice between alternatives affects business outcomes. It's not about the absolute stakes, but about relative differences in stakes. The key question is: How different will the results be if you choose one option over another? There might be cases where lots of money is at stake, but choosing one option over another doesn't significantly change the outcome, maybe because the options are very similar or the results are inevitable no matter which option you choose. In such instances, the importance of the decision remains low, even with high financial stakes.

For Question, 0 signifies low value, 1 stands for medium value, and 2 implies high value. Here value should be understood as value of information. A question has value when the answer greatly changes the confidence you have in choosing one option versus another.

For Data, a score of 0 means that the data needed to find out the answer is very hard or even impossible to find. A score of 1 indicates some difficulty in acquiring the data, while a score of 2 suggests data that can be easily obtained. The difficulty level depends on the resources needed to gather or analyze the data.

Looking at decision-driven analytics this way highlights a few key points:

- Companies should invest in projects where all components score high, because the multiplicative formula compounds the scores ($2 \times 2 \times 2 >>> 1 \times 1 \times 1 > 0 \times 0 \times 0$). These projects offer the opportunity to easily solve important problems, and they should be the priority of any business.
- The components of decision-driven analytics on the right side of the equation can balance each other out. For instance,

an answer might be tough to find, but if the decision is crucial enough, the company might still go after it.

- However, there's a limit to this compensatory process. If one component scores a zero, the overall score becomes zero, too. That means if any element suggests not to pursue analytics, the entire process stops.

Of course, these are simplified examples, a kind of mental exercise. But we recommend that companies adopt this way of thinking. It can help prioritize analytics projects and clarify assumptions. It can point out differences in understanding between different individuals, like data analysts and decision-makers, and overall improve communication and understanding.

Effective and Efficient

The primary goal of decision-driven analytics is to enhance a company's return on analytics investments by making such investments both effective and efficient. "Effective" here means that the analytics should bolster decision-making quality. "Efficient" instead means that this improvement should be achieved with minimal expenditure of time, money, and other resources.

Throughout this book, we've emphasized effectiveness, showcasing numerous examples of how decision-driven analytics can lead to superior outcomes and choices. However, implementing this approach isn't straightforward. It demands significant resources and thoughtful planning. It's neither practical nor productive to apply such a rigorous process to every single decision. That would be crippling.

Decision-driven analytics focuses on providing answers to assist decision-makers. Thus, companies should consider the value of pursuing these answers. There could be many reasons to forgo the answers. Decision-driven analytics is a strategic approach that emphasizes the alignment of analytical efforts with decision-making needs. However, before investing in such efforts, companies must evaluate the impact, relevance, and feasibility of the answers they seek.

The Thinking Trap

The Trap

Believe that doing more analytics is always good.

What It Looks Like . . .

Decision-makers say, "We should not make decisions without data."

The Antidote

Before engaging in data analytics, ask three questions: "Does it matter what we do?," "Will we choose wisely?," and "How much will it cost?"

The Takeaways

- It is not desirable to adopt a decision-driven analytics approach for every decision. Organizations need structured methods to prioritize their efforts. A series of three queries can guide this prioritization.

- Some decisions are not consequential enough to merit analytical efforts. Hence, the initial query is: "Does it matter what we do?"
- Not all questions are equally relevant. Distinguishing between relevant and irrelevant questions is challenging but crucial. The second query, therefore, is: "Will it help to make an informed decision?"
- While some data is readily accessible, procuring other data can be prohibitively expensive. The final query is: "How much will it cost to get an answer"?
- The assessment of these questions is compensatory; for example, a very important decision may justify substantial investments in analytics. However, there are boundaries. If the response to any question is resoundingly negative, it's a sign to forego analytics for that particular decision.

Conclusion
A New Division of Labor

During the Scientific Revolution, new technologies like the microscope and the telescope enabled scientists to unravel many mysteries of the natural world. For example, technology enabled improving our observations of the sky. Today, we are living another revolution, powered by artificial intelligence (AI).

Reading the news these days, one gets the impression that machines are taking over. Every day we hear about a new spectacular feat that AI has become capable of performing. We teach a course on AI in business and, every time we teach it, we must update the slides where we present examples of what AI struggles to do. The list of tasks that machines are unable to perform is shrinking fast—and our slide deck is shrinking with it. At the same time, the list of tasks where human performance is met or exceeded by machines, while shorter, is getting longer equally fast.

With AI getting better and better, many see ominous signs that our old carbon-based brains will soon become obsolete. Moving forward, they ask, what is going to be the value of human judgment in business decision-making? The conversation can quickly get quite dark, with frequent references to doomsday scenarios like *The Terminator* or *The Matrix*.

A Story About Uranus

In the mid-1850s, astronomers figured that the orbit of the planet Uranus was not like it should be according to the laws of physics. A French astronomer, Alexis Bouvard, thought that perhaps that was because we didn't know about a planet further out in the solar system that exerted an influence on Uranus's orbit. People started searching the sky for it. Soon enough, Urbain Le Verrier, another Frenchman, found the missing planet. It was named Neptune.

This was a great victory for the power of observation. Investing in data collection saved the day. It taught astronomers that the key to unraveling the mysteries of the cosmos was more and better data.

The rationale for making decisions with input from analytics rests on similar principles. Without data we navigate blind, while with data we can make decisions rooted in evidence. The implication is that good thinking means thinking with data.

The story doesn't end here, though. An anomaly was soon observed also in the orbit of another planet: Mercury. The same Urbain Le Verrier who had found Neptune now hypothesized the existence of a missing planet lying between Mercury and the Sun. He called this missing planet Vulcan. Again, people started looking for it, only this time nobody could find it. Astronomers kept looking for Vulcan in the subsequent decades but the missing planet remained missing, and the mystery of Mercury unsolved.

The anomaly in the orbit of Mercury could be explained only half a century later. The explanation had to wait for Albert Einstein's publication of a new theory of gravitation, called the theory of general relativity. This theory revolutionized our understanding of the universe by placing space and time in a four-dimensional continuum.

Although nobody knew that before Einstein entered the scene, all planetary orbits were in fact not conforming to Isaac Newton's laws. Nobody knew that because the difference between the predictions of the two theories are smaller and smaller as you move away from the Sun. Only in the case of Mercury, which is the planet closest to the Sun, the curvature in space-time caused by the mass of the Sun was large enough for the divergence between the predictions based on Newton's and Einstein's theories to be detected by the telescopes of the time.

The mystery of Mercury was solved in a very different way from the mystery of Uranus. While the latter could be solved with better observations, the former could only be solved with better theory, by thinking without data.

Managers are like astronomers, looking to solve problems and find solutions in a complex world, where data is abundant but often hard to make sense of. The message is clear: Data and algorithms are crucial to making good decisions. But human judgment and intelligence are crucial, too.

Human Judgment in the Age of Artificial Intelligence

Decision-driven analytics aims to improve the collaboration between decision-makers and data analysts. Similarly, we should also think about the balance between human and artificial intelligence. Instead of fearing AI dominance, leaders ought to leverage the unique strengths of both humans and machines to make informed decisions. The preceding chapters have highlighted various examples.

A crucial step in decision-driven analytics is determining potential courses of action. This determination is central, because it influences all subsequent steps. And it remains a uniquely human responsibility. What strategic choices are viable for achieving a specific business objective considering our resources, market standing, and company values? While algorithms can offer insights, they can't make these judgments for us. For instance, the suggested actions must resonate with the decision-makers' ethical values. AI can't dictate the morals one should uphold.

AI, with its capacity to process vast datasets and predict potential outcomes, brings undeniable value to the table. However, it lacks an inherent sense of right or wrong.

The data it uses might have biases, and while its output can offer valuable insights, the moral weight and implications of these insights still fall upon human shoulders to assess. When impactful decisions are taken, they come with the need for responsibility and accountability. Humans, bound by societal norms, legal systems, and moral codes, are accountable for their actions. AI, however beneficial, remains a tool and cannot shoulder moral responsibility.

We talked about the role of counterfactual questions and why understanding cause and effect matters when planning actions. Algorithms often fall short in these areas. Take digital advertising as an example. Many managers base their decisions on the prowess of targeting algorithms to pinpoint consumers most likely to click on an ad. However, the more pertinent question is: Which consumers are genuinely influenced by that ad?

Similarly, when addressing customer churn, the focus often centers on predicting which customers might leave, rather than identifying those who would be receptive to measures aimed at retaining them. A recurring theme in this book is the conflation between factual and counterfactual questions. This blurring of lines occurs when decision-makers mistakenly believe that models trained on historical data hold all the answers.

Pablo Picasso once aptly remarked, "Computers are useless. They can only give you answers." We love this quote because it subtly underscores where human intelligence's true value might reside in the age of AI. By and large, it won't be in offering answers to questions—that's a domain where we'll lean on machines more and more. Instead, the real merit of human intelligence will be in formulating new and important questions.

The Four Pillars of Decision-Driven Analytics

We started this book with a basic math problem, introducing the personas of "divers" and "runners." While divers love crunching numbers, runners are eager to push forward and make an impact. Given that organizations comprise both divers and runners, there is a frequent disconnect between data analytics and decision-making.

In fact, many companies are witnessing an expanding gap between data and decisions, even with the goal of being a "data-driven organization." The increasing complexity of data and algorithms can make it harder for decision-makers to collaborate with data analysts. For a business to thrive, it's essential for both groups to understand and value each other's expertise.

This book presents a novel approach to data analytics we call decision-driven analytics. We explored the rise of data-driven decision-making, its pitfalls, and ways to improve. Many businesses find themselves overwhelmed by the sheer volume of data at their disposal. Putting decisions firmly at the center of the analytics process can be transformative. Starting with decisions and working back to the data will improve the quality of decision-making, improve the collaboration between managers and data analysts, and ultimately foster an organizational culture that is action oriented and that prizes the quality of decisions over ego or politics.

Here's a recap of decision-driven analytics's four core principles:

1. **Decisions.** Identify controllable, relevant decision alternatives. Consider diverse perspectives and a wide array of solutions. Prioritize feasible and impactful alternatives to achieve important business outcomes.
2. **Questions.** Formulate precise questions that will help rank the identified decision alternatives. Ambiguous questions can lead to miscommunication and poor decisions.
3. **Data.** Evaluate the data-generating mechanism. While Big Data can be tempting, the emphasis should be on collecting relevant data.
4. **Answers.** When the earlier steps are done right, determining the best action becomes straightforward. Remember, acknowledging uncertainty and sidestepping overconfidence are key for informed decisions.

Decision-driven analytics is about making informed choices, not just processing data or flooding presentations with graphs. It emphasizes gleaning actionable insights from pertinent data. Embracing this approach means letting go of the notion that every data point is vital and not being distracted by the newest tools.

If you take only one lesson from this book, we hope it's this: Data is just a means to an end. What matters is the decisions we make.

Notes

1 Lawson, M. A., R. P. Larrick, and J. B. Soll, "When and Why People Perform Mindless Math," *Judgment and Decision Making* 17, no. 6 (2022): 1208–28.

2 De Langhe, B., S. Puntoni, and R. P. Larrick, "Linear Thinking in a Nonlinear World," *Harvard Business Review* 95, no. 3 (2017): 130–39; Larrick, R. P., and J. B. Soll, "The MPG Illusion," *Science* 320, no. 5883 (2017): 1593–94.

3 Reisenbichler, M., T. Reutterer, D. Schweidel, and D. Dan, "Supporting Content Marketing with Natural Language Generation," *Marketing Science* 41, no. 3 (2022): 441–52.

4 Vasal, A., S. Vohra, E. Payan, and Y. Seedat, *Closing the Value Gap: How to Become Data Driven and Pivot to the New* (Accenture, 2019).

5 Pastore, R., M. Spires, and C. Key, "Achieving IT Excellence in the Age of Digital Disruption," The Hackett Group (2020). Retrieved August 6, 2023, from https://links.imagerelay.com/cdn/2925/ql/577b1ffcecf74a7199993af9190ce742 /Hackett-2020-Key-Issues-IT-2001.pdf.

6 "Data and Analytics Leadership Annual Executive Survey 2023," NewVantage Partners (2023). Retrieved August 6, 2023, from https://www.wavestone.us/wp -content/uploads/2022/12/Design-2023-Data-Analytics-Survey-Report.pdf.

7 Fleming, O., T. Fountaine, N. Henke, and T. Saleh, "Ten Red Flags Signaling Your Analytics Program Will Fail," *McKinsey Quarterly* (May 2018). Retrieved August 6, 2023, from https://www.mckinsey.com/capabilities/quantumblack/our -insights/ten-red-flags-signaling-your-analytics-program-will-fail#/.

8 De Langhe, B., "Covid-19 Vaccine Trials Are a Case Study on the Challenges of Data Literacy," *Harvard Business Review* (2020). Retrieved August 8, 2023, from https://hbr.org/2020/12/covid-19-vaccine-trials-are-a-case-study-on-the -challenges-of-data-literacy.

9 Robbins, R., and B. Mueller, "After Admitting Mistake, AstraZeneca Faces Difficult Questions about Its Vaccine," *New York Times*, November 25, 2020, https://www.nytimes.com/2020/11/25/business/coronavirus-vaccine -astrazeneca-oxford.html.

10 Wikipedia, "Customer Attrition" (n.d.). Retrieved August 6, 2023, from https://en.wikipedia.org/wiki/Customer_attrition.

11 Sasser, W. E., and F. F. Reichheld, "Zero Defections: Quality Comes to Services," *Harvard Business Review* 68, no. 5 (1990): 105–11.

12　Ascarza, E., "Retention Futility: Targeting High-Risk Customers Might Be Ineffective," *Journal of Marketing Research* 55, no. 1 (2018): 80–98.

13　Dzyabura, D., S. El Kihal, J. R. Hauser, and M. Ibragimov, "Leveraging the Power of Images in Managing Product Return Rates," *Marketing Science* (2023), https://doi.org/10.1287/mksc.2023.1451.

14　Issenberg, S., *The Victory Lab: The Secret Science of Winning Campaigns* (Crown, 2012).

15　De Langhe, B., and S. Puntoni, "Facebook's Misleading Campaign against Apple's Privacy Policy," *Harvard Business Review* (2021), https://hbr.org/2021/02/facebooks-misleading-campaign-against-apples-privacy-policy.

16　De Langhe, B., and S. Puntoni, "Does Personalized Advertising Work as Well as Tech Companies Claim?" *Harvard Business Review* (2001). Retrieved August 8, 2023, from https://hbr.org/2021/12/does-personalized-advertising-work-as-well-as-tech-companies-claim.

17　Braun, M., B. De Langhe, S. Puntoni, and E. Schwartz, "Leveraging Digital Advertising Platforms for Consumer Research," *Journal of Consumer Research* (forthcoming).

18　Matz, S. C., M. Kosinski, G. Nave, and D. J. Stillwell, "Psychological Targeting as an Effective Approach to Digital Mass Persuasion," *Proceedings of the National Academy of Sciences* 114, no. 48 (2017): 12714–19.

19　Eckles, D., B. R. Gordon, and G. A. Johnson, "Field Studies of Psychologically Targeted Ads Face Threats to Internal Validity," *Proceedings of the National Academy of Sciences* 115, no. 23 (2018): E5254–55.

20　Morris, J., "Israeli Data: How Can Efficacy vs. Severe Disease Be Strong When 60% of Hospitalized Are Vaccinated?" *Covid-19 Data Science*, August 17, 2021, https://www.covid-datascience.com/post/israeli-data-how-can-efficacy-vs-severe-disease-be-strong-when-60-of-hospitalized-are-vaccinated.

21　Gordon, B. R., R. Moakler, and F. Zettelmeyer, "Close Enough? A Large-Scale Exploration of Non-experimental Approaches to Advertising Measurement," *Marketing Science* 42, no. 4 (2022): 768–93.

22　Vosgerau, J., "Big Data, Big Biases," YouTube, April 8, 2022, https://www.youtube.com/watch?v=UJzlMFx72q4.

23　"Tech Downturn Slashes Billions from Value of World's Most Valuable Brands," Brandirectory. Retrieved August 6, 2023, from https://brandirectory.com/rankings/global/.

24　Counts, A., and J. Levine, "Twitter Turning into X Set to Kill Billions in Brand Value," *Bloomberg*, July 24, 2023, https://www.bloomberg.com/news/articles/2023-07-24/twitter-turning-into-x-is-set-to-kill-billions-in-brand-value.

25　Retrieved August 6, 2023, from https://www.kantar.com/campaigns/brandz/global.

26 Hofman, J. M., D. G. Goldstein, and J. Hullman, "How Visualizing Inferential
    Uncertainty Can Mislead Readers about Treatment Effects in Scientific Results,"
    Proceedings of the 2020 Chi Conference on Human Factors in Computing Systems
    (April 2020), 1–12.

27 De Langhe, B., and P. M. F. Fernbach, "The Dangers of Categorical Thinking,"
    Harvard Business Review 97, no. 5 (2019): 80–92.

28 Stromberg, J., and E. Caswell, "Why the Myers–Briggs Test Is Totally
    Meaningless," *Vox*, October 8, 2015, https://www.vox.com/2014/7/15/5881947
    /myers-briggs-personality-test-meaningless.

29 Peter L. J., and R. Hull, *The Peter Principle: Why Things Always Go Wrong*
    (William Morrow, 1969).

30 Benson, A., D. Li, and K. Shue, "Promotions and the Peter Principle," *Quarterly
    Journal of Economics* 134, no. 4 (2019): 2085–134.

Index

Page numbers ending in *f* or *t* refer to figures or tables.

About the Authors

Bart De Langhe is a professor of marketing at KU Leuven and Vlerick Business School. He also founded Behavioral Economics and Data Analytics for Business (BEDAB), a consultancy that assists companies in using behavioral science and data analysis to make better decisions and improve performance. De Langhe's research examines how managers and consumers make judgments and decisions, with a specific emphasis on their intuitions about data, metrics, and statistics. He has published articles in leading academic journals in business and psychology, such as the *Journal of Marketing Research*; *Management Science*; the *Journal of Consumer Research*; and the *Journal of Experimental Psychology: General*. His work has also been featured in popular outlets, such as *Harvard Business Review*, *MIT Sloan Management Review*, the *Wall Street Journal*, and the *New York Times*. In 2017, he was recognized by the Marketing Science Institute as one of the most promising young scholars in marketing.

De Langhe has taught a wide array of courses related to marketing management, consumer behavior, behavioral economics, data analytics, and managerial decision-making at various academic levels, including undergraduate, MSc, MBA, EMBA, PhD, and open/custom executive programs. He has taught at prestigious business schools in Europe, North America, and Asia. As a testament to his excellence in teaching, De Langhe was recognized by Poets and

Quants in 2021 as a "best 40-under-40" business school professor. He received his PhD in marketing from Erasmus University, Rotterdam, and his bachelor's and master's degrees in psychology from KU Leuven.

Stefano Puntoni is the Sebastian S. Kresge Professor of Marketing at the Wharton School, University of Pennsylvania. He is also the codirector of AI at Wharton, an initiative to foster, coordinate, and promote research and teaching on artificial intelligence across the Wharton School.

Puntoni brings a behavioral science perspective to artificial intelligence and algorithms to investigate how automation is changing consumption and society. His research has appeared in many leading journals, including *Journal of Consumer Research*, *Journal of Marketing Research*, *Journal of Marketing*, *Journal of Consumer Psychology*, *Nature Human Behavior*, and *Management Science*. He also writes regularly for managerial outlets such as *Harvard Business Review* and *MIT Sloan Management Review*. He is a former MSI Young Scholar and MSI Scholar, and the winner of several grants and awards. Puntoni is currently an associate editor at the *Journal of Consumer Research* and at the *Journal of Marketing*.

At Wharton, Puntoni teaches undergraduates, MBAs, and executives in the areas of new technologies, marketing strategy, brand management, and decision-making. He holds a PhD in marketing from London Business School and a degree in statistics from the University of Padova in his native Italy. Prior to joining Penn he was a professor of marketing and department head at the Rotterdam School of Management, Erasmus University, in the Netherlands.

About Wharton School Press

Wharton School Press, the book publishing arm of the Wharton School of the University of Pennsylvania, was established to inspire bold, insightful thinking within the global business community.

An imprint of University of Pennsylvania Press, Wharton School Press publishes a select list of award-winning, bestselling, and thought-leading books that offer trusted business knowledge to help leaders at all levels meet the challenges of today and the opportunities of tomorrow. Led by a spirit of innovation and experimentation, Wharton School Press leverages groundbreaking digital technologies and has pioneered a fast-reading business book format that fits readers' busy lives, allowing them to swiftly emerge with the tools and information needed to make an impact. Wharton School Press books offer guidance and inspiration on a variety of topics, including leadership, management, strategy, innovation, entrepreneurship, finance, marketing, social impact, public policy, and more.

To find books that will inspire and empower you to increase your impact and expand your personal and professional horizons, visit wsp.wharton.upenn.edu.

UNIVERSITY *of* **PENNSYLVANIA**

About the Wharton School

Founded in 1881 as the world's first collegiate business school, the Wharton School of the University of Pennsylvania is shaping the future of business by incubating ideas, driving insights, and creating leaders who change the world. With a faculty of more than 235 renowned professors, Wharton has 5,000 undergraduate, MBA, executive MBA, and doctoral students. Each year 13,000 professionals from around the world advance their careers through Wharton Executive Education's individual, company-customized, and online programs. More than 100,000 Wharton alumni form a powerful global network of leaders who transform business every day.

www.wharton.upenn.edu

About Penn Press

True to its Philadelphia roots, Penn Press is well known for its distinguished list of publications in American history and culture, including innovative work on the transnational currents that surrounded and shaped the republic from the colonial period through the present, as well as prize-winning publications in urban studies. The Press is equally renowned for its publications in European history, literature, and culture from late antiquity through the early modern period. Penn Press's social science publications tackle contemporary political issues of concern to a broad readership of citizens and scholars, notably including a long-standing commitment to publishing path-breaking work in international human rights. Penn Press also publishes outstanding works in archaeology, economic history, business, and Jewish studies in partnership with local institutions.

You can learn more about our recent publications by visiting www.pennpress.org or viewing our seasonal catalogs.

Printed in the USA
CPSIA information can be obtained
at www.ICGtesting.com
JSHW082146210224
57798JS00003B/6